Welfare

Other Books in the Social Issues Firsthand Series:

AIDS

Body Piercing and Tattoos

Child Abuse and Neglect

Cults

Date and Acquaintance Rape

Drunk Driving

Eating Disorders

Gangs

Prostitution

Sexual Predators

Teenage Pregnancy

Welfare

Katherine Swarts, Book Editor

GREENHAVEN PRESS
A part of Gale, Cengage Learning

Detroit • New York • San Francisco • New Haven, Conn • Waterville, Maine • London

Christine Nasso, *Publisher*
Elizabeth Des Chenes, *Managing Editor*

© 2008 Greenhaven Press, a part of Gale, Cengage Learning

For more information, contact:
Greenhaven Press
27500 Drake Rd.
Farmington Hills, MI 48331-3535
Or you can visit our Internet site at gale.cengage.com

ALL RIGHTS RESERVED
No part of this work covered by the copyright herein may be reproduced, transmitted, stored, or used in any form or by any means graphic, electronic, or mechanical, including but not limited to photocopying, recording, scanning, digitizing, taping, Web distribution, information networks, or information storage retrieval systems, except as permitted under Section 107 or 108 of the 1976 United States Copyright Act, without the prior written permission of the publisher.

For product information and technology assistance, contact us at

Gale Customer Support, 1-800-877-4253
For permission to use material from this text or product, submit all requests online at
www.cengage.com/permissions

Further permissions questions can be emailed to permissionrequest@cengage.com

Articles in Greenhaven Press anthologies are often edited for length to meet page requirements. In addition, original titles of these works are changed to clearly present the main thesis and to explicitly indicate the author's opinion. Every effort is made to ensure that Greenhaven Press accurately reflects the original intent of the authors. Every effort has been made to trace the owners of copyrighted material.

Cover photograph reproduced by permission of AP Images.

LIBRARY OF CONGRESS CATALOGING-IN-PUBLICATION DATA

Welfare / Katherine Swarts, book editor.
  p. cm. -- (Social issues firsthand)
  Includes bibliographical references and index.
  ISBN-13: 978-0-7377-4079-0 (hardcover)
  1. Public welfare--United States--Juvenile literature. I. Swarts, Katherine.
  HV91.W4663 2008
  362.5'560973--dc22
                                                                    2008006571

Printed in the United States of America
1 2 3 4 5 6 7 12 11 10 09 08

Contents

Foreword   9

Introduction   12

Chapter 1: Welfare Recipients and Applicants

1. A Welfare Family In a New Neighborhood   16
   Mary Childers

   The daughter of a poor, white, single mother who "fit the stereotype of a welfare queen" recalls her large family's struggle to find decent housing and to cope with crime and urban deterioration.

2. My Mother Was Jailed for Welfare Fraud   22
   James E. Rogan

   A teenager sees his mother serve jail time because she broke a "no jobs while on welfare" law to provide for her family—and admitted she would do it again.

3. Being on Welfare Has Taught Me About Racism   26
   Rebecca Hensley

   A former welfare recipient, now a college professor, recalls what she learned about differences between typical experiences of whites and blacks on welfare—and in the larger society.

4. A Longtime Welfare Recipient Looks at the System   31
   Sugar Turner and Tracy Bachrach Ehlers

   An African American former welfare mother, having taken her anthropologist coauthor on a "guided tour" of the local Family Opportunity office, provides an insider's view on what it means to maintain one's dignity while in the system.

5. The Problems with Reformed Welfare   36
   Karen Seccombe

   A sociologist collects comments from welfare recipients on what still needs reforming since 1996.

Chapter 2: Other Perspectives on Welfare

1. Working in Human Services Is Rewarding 43
   Ana Pagan

   Having been employed for more than twenty-five years in jobs that assist the poor and disadvantaged, the director of the Merced County Human Services Agency discusses the rewards and vision of her work.

2. Investigating How the New Welfare Works 46
   Sharon Hays

   The author of *Flat Broke with Children: Women in the Age of Welfare Reform* describes her experiences researching the book.

3. Welfare and Child Care 57
   Gina Adams

   A senior research associate in the Urban Institute's Center on Labor, Human Services, and Population discusses how to provide effective child-care subsidies for welfare-to-work parents.

4. Waiting at a Welfare Office 64
   Karen Wilhelm

   Sent to the local welfare office for a background check as part of a volunteer approval process, the writer observes firsthand the frustrations applicants are subjected to.

Chapter 3: Creating Welfare Policy

1. From Civil Rights to Welfare Rights 70
   Marian Kramer, as told to Alan Govenar

   A longtime civil rights and antipoverty activist describes her work with the National Welfare Rights Union to ensure fair laws and equal opportunities.

2. The Struggle to Pass Welfare Reform 79
   Ron Haskins

   A veteran of fourteen years on the U.S. House of Representatives' Ways and Means Resources Subcommittee recounts the 1996 legislative struggle to pass a major welfare reform bill after two previous attempts were vetoed.

3. Encouraging Welfare Recipients to Take   **93**
   Responsibility for Their Future
   George W. Bush

   The president of the United States speaks on the welfare reforms of the late 1990s and their effects on employment among welfare recipients.

4. The Food Stamp Program Benefits   **98**
   Low-Income Children
   Nancy Montanez Johner

   The undersecretary of food, nutrition, and consumer services, U.S. Department of Agriculture, testifies before Congress on the value of food stamp benefits in ensuring healthy nutrition for low-income children and on her section's work to make people aware of these benefits.

Organizations to Contact	**107**
For Further Research	**112**
Index	**117**

Foreword

Social issues are often viewed in abstract terms. Pressing challenges such as poverty, homelessness, and addiction are viewed as problems to be defined and solved. Politicians, social scientists, and other experts engage in debates about the extent of the problems, their causes, and how best to remedy them. Often overlooked in these discussions is the human dimension of the issue. Behind every policy debate over poverty, homelessness, and substance abuse, for example, are real people struggling to make ends meet, to survive life on the streets, and to overcome addiction to drugs and alcohol. Their stories are ubiquitous and compelling. They are the stories of everyday people—perhaps your own family members or friends—and yet they rarely influence the debates taking place in state capitols, the national Congress, or the courts.

The disparity between the public debate and private experience of social issues is well illustrated by looking at the topic of poverty. Each year the U.S. Census Bureau establishes a poverty threshold. A household with an income below the threshold is defined as poor, while a household with an income above the threshold is considered able to live on a basic subsistence level. For example, in 2003 a family of two was considered poor if its income was less than $12,015; a family of four was defined as poor if its income was less than $18,810. Based on this system, the bureau estimates that 35.9 million Americans (12.5 percent of the population) lived below the poverty line in 2003, including 12.9 million children below the age of eighteen.

Commentators disagree about what these statistics mean. Social activists insist that the huge number of officially poor Americans translates into human suffering. Even many families that have incomes above the threshold, they maintain, are likely to be struggling to get by. Other commentators insist that the statistics exaggerate the problem of poverty in the United States. Compared to people in developing countries, they point out, most so-called poor families have a high quality of life. As stated by journalist Fidelis Iyebote, "Cars are owned by 70 percent of 'poor' households.... Color televisions belong to 97 percent of the 'poor' [and] videocassette recorders belong to nearly 75 percent.... Sixty-four percent have microwave ovens, half own a stereo system, and over a quarter possess an automatic dishwasher."

However, this debate over the poverty threshold and what it means is likely irrelevant to a person living in poverty. Simply put, poor people do not need the government to tell them whether they are poor. They can see it in the stack of bills they cannot pay. They are aware of it when they are forced to choose between paying rent or buying food for their children. They become painfully conscious of it when they lose their homes and are forced to live in their cars or on the streets. Indeed, the written stories of poor people define the meaning of poverty more vividly than a government bureaucracy could ever hope to. Narratives composed by the poor describe losing jobs due to injury or mental illness, depict horrific tales of childhood abuse and spousal violence, recount the loss of friends and family members. They evoke the slipping away of social supports and government assistance, the descent into substance abuse and addiction, the harsh realities of life on the streets. These are the perspectives on poverty that are too often omitted from discussions over the extent of the problem and how to solve it.

Greenhaven Press's Social Issues Firsthand series provides a forum for the often-overlooked human perspectives on society's most divisive topics of debate. Each volume focuses on one social issue and presents a collection of ten to sixteen narratives by those who have had personal involvement with the topic. Extra care has been taken to include a diverse range of perspectives. For example, in the volume on adoption, readers will find the stories of birth parents who have made an adoption plan, adoptive parents, and adoptees themselves. After exposure to these varied points of view, the reader will have a clearer understanding that adoption is an intense, emotional experience full of joyous highs and painful lows for all concerned.

The debate surrounding embryonic stem cell research illustrates the moral and ethical pressure that the public brings to bear on the scientific community. However, while nonexperts often criticize scientists for not considering the potential negative impact of their work, ironically the public's reaction against such discoveries can produce harmful results as well. For example, although the outcry against embryonic stem cell research in the United States has resulted in fewer embryos being destroyed, those with Parkinson's, such as actor Michael J. Fox, have argued that prohibiting the development of new stem cell lines ultimately will prevent a timely cure for the disease that is killing Fox and thousands of others.

Each book in the series contains several features that enhance its usefulness, including an in-depth introduction, an annotated table of contents, bibliographies for further research, a list of organizations to contact, and a thorough index. These elements—combined with the poignant voices of people touched by tragedy and triumph—make the Social Issues Firsthand series a valuable resource for research on today's topics of political discussion.

Introduction

Asked whether the United States should assist its poor and disadvantaged citizens, most Americans would likely answer, "Of course." But mention the word *welfare*, and those same Americans may have completely different, often negative reactions. For many, the misconception that most welfare recipients are unwilling to work is still strong.

Fully Employed and Still Poor

Should all welfare recipients be required to work, as per current welfare laws based on the Personal Responsibility and Work Opportunity Reconciliation Act of 1996? And when welfare recipients do find jobs, will this necessarily be a way out of the poverty that put them on welfare in the first place?

Considering the correlation between salary and education level, and the fact that only about half of welfare recipients even finished high school, there are definite problems with the idea that welfare recipients simply need to get jobs. Nearly all work readily available to typical recipients (single women with limited education) involves housekeeping or janitorial duties, or customer service in low-priced stores and restaurants—all of which pay minimum or near-minimum wage. And such jobs also tend to require hours that interfere with attempts to explore other opportunities.

In 1999, millions of women were "being pushed into the labor market by welfare reform," writes journalist Barbara Ehrenreich, who thus began an investigation to "find out just how they were going to survive on the wages of the unskilled—at $6 to $7 an hour, only half of what is considered a living wage."

The World of a Low-Wage Worker

Presenting herself as a recently divorced former homemaker, Ehrenreich took jobs as a restaurant server in Florida, a cleaning woman in Maine, and a sales clerk in Minnesota. She learned firsthand how many welfare-level women live with regular condescension and unfair treatment from employers, work extra jobs to keep from becoming homeless, and do without such middle-class basics as refrigerators and health insurance. Her resulting book, *Nickel and Dimed: On (Not) Getting By in America*, made the *New York Times* best seller list.

"[I was shocked by] the totalitarian nature of so many low-wage workplaces," recalls Ehrenreich. "I struggled to learn the computer ordering systems in restaurants, to memorize the names and dietary restrictions of thirty Alzheimer's patients, and, at WalMart, to memorize the exact locations of all the items in ladies' wear—which would then be rotated every few days.... When I got an uncontrollably itchy rash on the housecleaning job, probably from the cleaning fluids[,] I thought I should go to an emergency room [ER] if I wanted to remain 'in character,' but I was afraid I'd lose the job if I took a day off to do that.... What I didn't know at the time is that an ER visit would have been out of the question anyway, since they cost about $1000 on average, or a month's pay on this job.... I was angry about poverty before, but now I am in a permanent, low-level, rage."

Individuals, Not Objects

Others echo Ehrenreich's frustration with the welfare system's current emphasis on finding jobs. Many have more serious worries than skin rashes or brain-twisting work requirements. "[One] potential welfare client ... was the full-time caregiver for her grandchild on a lung machine, her terminally ill father, and her own two young children," reports Sharon Hays, a sociology professor who has done extensive research on the human side of welfare. "In order to receive benefits she would need to begin a job search immediately. [But] no one else was available to care for her father or grandchild."

Welfare

All this is closely related to another common complaint of welfare recipients—that they're treated as objects or problems, not as individuals with unique difficulties and needs. Likewise, the social workers who struggle with their duties, the politicians who genuinely try to consider the needs involved, and even the journalists who take the trouble to look at things firsthand, may be ignored by the average American who prefers to turn a blind eye to the whole subject of welfare.

It is those frequently overlooked voices that speak in this book.

CHAPTER 1

Welfare Recipients and Applicants

A Welfare Family in a New Neighborhood

Mary Childers

Mary Childers grew up in the 1960s, one of seven children with a welfare-dependent, white, single mother. Today, Childers is a conflict mediator and discrimination-prevention consultant with a PhD in English literature. In her memoir, Welfare Brat, *from which the following selection is excerpted, she recounts her turbulent early years and her determination to escape the generational cycle of poverty.*

The excerpt recounts a period when she was about twelve years old, and her family moved to an apartment in a formerly well-to-do neighborhood now turning dilapidated and dangerous in the wake of "white flight." Childers describes the struggle to adjust and her cynicism over a world where it seems everything deteriorates just as she discovers it.

When Mom stopped drinking, she started planning again. Acknowledging that the two-bedroom Shakespeare Avenue apartment [in New York City] was too small for us and that the landlord would never correct the frequent flooding in the apartment above, she undertook a quest for an affordable three-bedroom. Grateful for leads from neighbors, she hounded local landlords who were torn between their reluctance to shelter welfare families and to forgo rent on apartments abandoned by white flight. Soon after [my sister] Alice's birthday, we moved into a grand three-bedroom apartment on the top of a hill overlooking a park just five blocks from Shakespeare Avenue.

The move was an ordeal Mom still hasn't recovered from a month later. Her black and blue marks show no signs of fad-

Mary Childers, *Welfare Brat*. London: Bloomsbury Publishing, 2005. Copyright © 2005 by Mary Childers. All rights reserved. Reproduced by permission.

ing and she curls her shoulders forward to reduce the pain. Dana [the female romantic partner of my sister Lacey], Lacey, Jackie and Mom had spent two days dragging furniture up the hill on a dolly and then up the stairs to our new place. The rest of us hauled empty drawers, cushions and boxes of clothes and kitchen supplies.

A Hodgepodge of Secondhand Furnishings

As each big piece of furniture settled against a wall, Mom reminisced about its origins. "It's French. Hard to believe someone would give away a piece with so much detail. It takes blood, sweat and tears to carve flowers without the wood splitting." I chiseled into her good mood by pointing to unmatched knobs and the drawer that wouldn't close all the way. Despite years of promising not to collect any more heavy furniture, Mom can't pass up a bargain at Goodwill or a chest of drawers abandoned on the street for the first comer.

We rode our seesaw of gratitude and complaint until it was time for balance and levelheadedness to link us. Mom conceded on the effect of the hodgepodge of styles. "We're living in a secondhand store!"

I yielded, in turn. "You're right; wood furniture beats plywood." She made me admit that sometimes the grain and design of a particular piece of furniture make it worth lugging around, but I had to add: "as long as we stay put for a while."

Lacey and Dana seconded my prayer. "Amen!" They had been real sports, helping Mom pack and then carrying the heaviest furniture themselves, proud of their strength. "Who needs a man when you're already a workhorse?"

Assigning Bedrooms

Mom insists on sleeping in the living room so that her [five older] girls can have the two big bedrooms and her boy a small room all to himself. Emma [the youngest] encamps in a crib near the couch, so there's almost always someone to play with her. Because Jackie, in Mom's lingo, rarely deigns to visit, Alice enjoys the privacy I crave; Mom still checks on her several times a night without knocking. [Alice had nearly died after being hit by a car some months earlier.] Despite Alice's growing hair and body, Mom fears that some surprise brain activity may hijack Alice's life while she sleeps.

[My sister] Joan and I love the room we share. The former tenants left painted shutters on our two sets of floor-to-ceiling windows. Finally, we are princesses. From the streets Joan yells up at me to let out my golden brown hair, and I dangle a rope with messages all the way down the four flights. Late at night we still soothe each other with protestations of Best Friends Forever, but we're most transported by songs about everlasting love.

A Shabby and Violent Neighborhood

Settling into the apartment turns out to be easier than getting used to the building and our block. On nights when the radiators spew too much heat, the kids walk around in underwear. I itch with discomfort because my modesty keeps me covered, as if, I'm teased, I have something to hide. We crack open the windows and submit to noises that steal the sweetness from our dreams. People blast stereos without regard for neighbors, and no one dares object. Addicts snooze all day and exercise their lungs at night, bellowing greetings, curses and deal breakers. The thunder of bongos and lightning threats of gang members bolt across the street from the park, where Puerto Ricans and blacks have staked out different sections. Irish cops out of uniform sometimes show up to instigate fights over who owns the swings and basketball courts. Dominicans increase tension by elbowing the space of the Puerto Ricans. The more people fight, the less there is to fight over. When it's cold, the night owls and party people burn benches that are never replaced; the city no longer bothers to clean the park bathrooms.

My first association with a knife is that it is a weapon, not a utensil. I close my eyes tightly, like the shutters on my bedroom windows, when I remember the streaks of blood in the hall where an elderly woman unwisely clutched her purse against the demands of a knife-wielding punk. But knives are falling out of fashion. Increasingly, guns are what we should fear.

Will Joan Ever Grow Up?

With the park off limits, Joan spends hours on the sidewalk outside the house. One Saturday I leave for my tutoring session with Sally and Norah [twin sisters in the neighborhood, both of whom have Down syndrome and whose parents hired me as a teacher] after teasing her for playing hopscotch with kids three years younger than herself. When I return several hours later, she is still there, jumping rope and chalking up the sidewalk with eight-year-olds. In front of her new friends, I yell that she should grow up and help Mom with the laundry on a Saturday instead of playing like a baby. Chalk marks on her butt and dirt smudged on her reddened face, she sprays me like a bursting fountain of wisdom: "What's so good about growing up? Boys bother you and you're expected to be clean all the time."

I leave her alone because I'm wiped out from my tutoring, which consists mostly of wrestling the twins for attention despite knowing they forget everything I teach them within two weeks. I have to believe there is hope for Joan, but I'm worried. She jumps at the chance to stay home from school and would watch cartoons all day every day if she could. As if she's still a little girl, she carries her Chatty Cathy doll around to start conversations with other kids on our block, viewing everyone as a potential friend.

No Safe Place near Home

The graffiti-scarred halls of our building are almost as dangerous as the park. If bad weather hits, punks from the park seek shelter inside surrounding buildings. When we were moving in, we couldn't leave anything unattended for even a second. We played a relay game to safely deliver everything we owned while creepy guys smoked weed under the stairs, occasionally coming out from under to check us out and slur welcomes. "That's a lot of sisters." "Who teaching that boy [Ralph, the only brother] to be a man?" "We'd help if we could stand, ladies."

The first day we were moving in, Joan, Alice and Ralph played hide-and-seek in the corridors connecting the two main entrances. But they quickly learned to use only the main entrance near the stairwell leading to our apartment. Even though the lock on the vestibule door is broken, we press the bell as soon as we enter the hall, speak into the intercom as if an adult has responded to our ring, and then hightail it upstairs. I may not believe in God, but I believe in boogeymen.

Haunted by Fear

I sense them everywhere in the long walks I take around the West Bronx, haunted by rumors of gang rapes that don't make the papers. I hope people are exaggerating our jeopardy. The rumble of trucks moving white people away from the neighborhood leaves me feeling as abandoned as when my father split. It turns out I inaccurately predicted what I would most miss about the Cranfords [a family I spent several summers with in upstate New York]. It's not the bedroom or the food; it's feeling safe meandering or biking through the streets. How could we not have known that we were moving uphill to danger? No one warned Mom that the sliver of green space we admired from our windows was the territory of untended, noxious human weeds. We're sinking in the same swamp as the rest of the regular folks who live here: Puerto Rican, black, Jewish, Irish and Italian families attached to spacious, affordable apartments and the neighborhoods that surround them. Once intimately linked to Manhattan by a stately bridge from the nineteenth century that gave this area the name Highbridge, our isolation and demise are now represented by that defunct, crumbling structure, closed even to foot traffic now in order to deter crime.

An old lady who moved here in the fifties and now is afraid to leave her apartment at night tells us that this neighborhood was once like a suburb, only better. You could rent big apartments with views and skip the worry of maintaining a house. "The West Bronx was part of the Art Deco [a popular ultra modern and elegant decorative style of the 1920s and 1930s] movement," she says, and I wonder when the decks crumbled and disappeared. She rambles on about a design craze for apartment homes that would ease the domestic burden on women. "Now Riverdale [in the northwest] is the part of the Bronx the wealthy choose."

Prophets of Urban Decay

Wouldn't you know that neighborhoods deteriorate just as we discover them? We're the John the Baptists of Urban Decay, alerting our fellow man to what's coming. Once the white trash moves in, it's nothing but poor colored families after that. Then landlords stop making repairs and building inspectors go blind, even though these buildings are worth fighting for in a way our old tenement wasn't. Because of vandalism and theft, Catholic churches now barricade their doors except when they are holding Mass. It figures that churches are closed most of the time just when my Mom has returned to the fold.

Lobbies in distant neighborhoods, like Riverdale, have become my churches. Instead of votive candles and illuminated altars, some glow from fireplaces with electric logs. I have staked out a few where people don't balk at my sitting quietly and reading as if I'm in my own living room. When I'm hot from walking, if no one is around I rip open my jacket, lift my shirt and crush my chest against the cool marble walls.

My Mother Was Jailed for Welfare Fraud

James E. Rogan

James E. Rogan grew up in the poor neighborhoods of the San Francisco Bay area, the oldest child of a mother who was single and on welfare during much of that time. He eventually became a Los Angeles County district attorney, later serving as a U.S. congressman (1997–2001) and subsequently (2001–2004) as undersecretary of commerce and director of the U.S. Patent and Trademark Office. A judge for the Superior Court of California since 2006, he received a 2007 presidential nomination to the United States District Court, Central District of California.

The incident recounted in this selection took place in the mid-1970s, when Rogan was a high school dropout in his late teens. His mother, while on welfare, had failed to report income from employment for fear that her assistance payments would be cut to the point where her total income would be again inadequate. Arrested for welfare fraud, she admitted in court that she would do it again, if necessary, to support her children—and she spent four months in jail as a result.

At a dance one night Mom met Jose, an easygoing, middle-aged Filipino working as a supervisor for the BART commuter trains. They dated for a while and then married. Theirs was never a "head over heels" love; they were more like good friends deciding to give marriage a try. It didn't last; their decision to split up came as casually as the one to marry: no fuss, nobody hurt, and ending as it began—friends. Still, Mom benefited from their brief marriage by saying goodbye to the

---

James E. Rogan, *Rough Edges: My Unlikely Road from Welfare to Washington*. New York: Regan Books, 2004. Copyright © 2004 by James E. Rogan. All rights reserved. Reproduced by permission of HarperCollins Publishers Inc.

welfare culture of Pinole. We moved to Livermore, a small city in a rural valley near Oakland. In the mid-1970s housing tracts were just beginning to pop up among the Livermore orchards and farmlands. Lawrence Livermore Lab, where they designed and tested nuclear bombs, was the valley's major employer. The big joke among residents was that if the Soviets ever attacked America, nobody in Livermore would know, since the first atomic strike would be against us.

A wrinkle developed after Mom's marriage: During her time on welfare, she took side jobs as a toy store cashier to make ends meet. The welfare check didn't provide enough for her large brood. Knowing the government would slash her benefits if she took a job, Mom didn't report it. Shortly after marrying Jose and moving to Livermore, an investigator showed up to question her about this old case. When she told the truth, the police booked her for welfare fraud.

Mom rejected her defense attorney's advice to plead "not guilty" and get a bargaining chip with the DA [district attorney]. Since the charges were true, she wanted to fess up and put the issue behind her. She pled guilty, and the judge told her to return in a few weeks for sentencing. Mom's lawyer reassured her the standard sentence in first-time cases like this was probation and restitution, with no jail time. When she returned to court for her sentencing, Mom watched a parade of welfare-cheating women take their turn before the judge. The litany never changed: The women wept, apologized, and in response to the judge's question, promised never to do it again. Each received the standard minimum sentence. When Mom's turn came, she skipped the tears but otherwise followed suit: She said she did it, she was sorry, and she wanted to pay back the money with interest. However, when the judge asked if she would do it again, Mom veered from the script. Wanting to be candid, she told the court, "Well, judge, in all honesty, if I needed to do it to keep my family together, then I guess I would."

Wrong answer: Like the other women, Mom received probation and was ordered to pay restitution; unlike the others, the judge sent her to jail. Mom spent about four months in custody, dividing her jail time between Martinez County Jail and a work furlough halfway house in Oakland. Meanwhile, Jose and I held down the fort.

Doris Derby, Mom's high school friend, told me not to worry about her being in jail: "Your mother's *always* been a tough broad." Up to now Mom never appeared fazed by difficult circumstances, but jail could depress even the most buoyant spirit. I didn't know what to expect when I saw her there the first time. I entered the visitor's area, which looked like a large recreation room. Mom wasn't hard to pick out of the crowd: She was the only white inmate there. Wearing a standard-issue jail jumpsuit, she chatted merrily with her jailers and fellow inmates while crocheting a rug. Her eyes lit up when she saw me, and after exchanging hugs she introduced me to her new companions. There was Mary, who had torched her motor home for the insurance money. Next to her was doper Debbie, for whom Mom later got a job at King Norman's Toy Store at Eastmont Mall. Mom also introduced me to Annie, who taught Mom how to crochet: "Annie stabbed her boyfriend—or did you shoot him, Annie? I can't remember." A wispy woman with a shy grin, Annie rolled her eyes as if embarrassed by the fuss. With doe-like innocence, she peeked up and cooed, "I sticked him."

"Oh, well" Mom shrugged, "it doesn't matter. He was a no-good son of a bitch anyway." Then Mom introduced me to a giggly jailer from whom she bummed a smoke. "We've heard so much about you!" the mountainous female guard said. "And we just love your Mom!" I felt like I'd stumbled into a family reunion.

The county later sent Mom eventually to a work furlough program that allowed her to leave jail for her day job; she spent only nights in custody for the remainder of her sentence. For most middle-aged women, jail would be an inducement into clinical depression. For Mom, it wasn't much more than an inconvenience. Her friend Doris was right: Mom was a tough broad.

Being on Welfare Has Taught Me About Racism

Rebecca Hensley

The author is a middle-aged, full-time writer who has worked as a college professor and sociologist. While her upbringing was primarily white middle-class, she spent five years on welfare as an independent adult, and has considerable personal experience (from childhood on) with being poorer than her immediate neighbors or the average white American. Her blog, "Why Am I Not Surprised?" deals with race relations and American diversity issues.

*In this essay, she discusses the concept of "hustling" to survive, as it relates to white and black people. Recalling a white social worker's remark some years earlier—"At least you don't have racism to deal with, too"—and a black man's comment that his race itself "*is a *hustle," she concludes that most black Americans still deal with considerably more uncertainty and mistrust than do whites.*

Back in my thirties, when I was on welfare for five years, before I got my bachelor's degree and my master's degree and the additional 82 graduate level hours I earned at FSU [Florida State University] working toward my Ph.D., when somebody asked me how I was making it, somebody African-American usually, since a European-American wouldn't ask, I used to reply, "I *hustle.*" And they would invariably laugh out loud. Not like they found it funny, but like they found it funny that I would use that word. It seemed as if maybe they thought I wouldn't know *how* to hustle. Or maybe that a White person wouldn't ever really *have* to hustle—even a

Rebecca Hensley, "Why Am I Not Surprised?: Hustle and Flow," *whyaminotsurprised*.*blogspot.com*, April 16, 2006. Reproduced by permission.

White person on welfare. Or at least that if I was, in fact, somehow "hustling," that they couldn't imagine me using the word appropriately. They laughed as if the word itself sounded funny coming out of my mouth.

Life Was One Hustle After Another

But I knew the word. By that time, I had been fully bi-cultural for at least several years and crossing the color line back and forth for more than a decade. I meant "hustle." I was living on barely over $300 per month and a handful of food stamps, after all, and even after I moved into subsidized housing (which was just one part of my hustle, once my friend Esther showed me how to get in), I was endlessly living on the edge. So any given day, I was liable to be "working it" one way or the other. Because I had to. White or not. My kids needed shoes. My son needed money for school projects. There were birthdays and Christmases and Easter baskets. Not to mention laundry to be done and toilet paper and toothpaste to be bought. Three hundred dollars just wasn't gonna do it. So I hustled.

Sometimes, I hustled a man, somebody I was dating who wanted my undivided attention. I didn't think of it as degrading. I just needed to cover all my bases, that's all. The utility company didn't want to hear about my rickety old junker breaking down. Heck! The car itself had been the result of a hustle. And God knows, I needed it, even if the driver's seat *was* tipped hard to the left as the floor disintegrated underneath it. I had responsibilities just like every other adult, Black or White. And whatever it took within reason, I met them.

Hustling After Welfare

It didn't stop when I got off welfare either. For seven years of grad school, I hustled my way through student loans and financial aid and assistantships and summer jobs and endlessly through family and friends and boyfriends and even a husband or two. Even after I left school and went to work full-time, it seemed as if I was always a dollar or two (or more) shy of where I wanted—and often needed—to be. I had teenagers to support and inflation to deal with, of course, as well as the tendency to make an odd choice from time to time. And everybody gets a bad break now and then, such as being laid off from a great job after only six months because of programmatic cut-backs—two days after my druggie son and his girlfriend "had to" move in without jobs themselves. I mean, it was *always* something.

And for the most part, it still is. Granted, I *chose* to quit my day-job eighteen months ago to write, a choice that a number of my friends and acquaintances considered crazy. But I'm used to living on a wing and a prayer most of the time *anyway* and I was just taking a calculated risk, trying to hustle my way into the place I think I *really* belong, if you catch my drift.

Brought Face to Face with the Race Issue

Still, I remember one winter in northern Illinois back in the day going to a Community Action Agency to ask for help with my utility bill. I was crying the blues, I guess, whining about whatever my current struggle was (hustling, hustling) when the European-American woman caseworker on the other side of the desk said abruptly, "Well, at least you're *White*, so you don't have *racism* to deal with, too."

I was *shocked*. Shocked that she would speak to me like that when she was supposed to be a "social worker." Shocked that she would speak to me about how being White makes you special when she was White, *too*. Shocked, as a matter of fact, that she would talk about Whiteness at *all*, since only Black folks talked about White folks being White back then. And shocked, I think, that she did this with no apparent emotional investment at all. She was just saying it *straight out*. It shut down my hustle like a glass of cold water in the face.

"Bein' Black Is a Hustle"

Anyway, all this went through my mind a few weeks ago, after I had a conversation with a young African-American student who was telling me about his fledgling business in the entertainment field. He was explaining how it's against the law to post flyers in public, but that the cops will allow them in the Black community if you don't get caught putting them up. So they go out after dark to post advertisements about their next event. They dress in black, in cheap shoes, and without a watch or a wallet or even a jacket, so as not to tempt the local roadboys, who might be out marauding.

"You can't look like you have anything or they'll getcha," he said. "And you can't ride a bike after dark or you'll wind up in a fight. The rule is: if you can't defend what you have, you don't deserve it."

I looked into his eyes, as he matter-of-factly recounted the adventure. "In a capitalist society," he finished, "money is the equalizer." I didn't know if he was talking about himself or the roadboys . . . or both. And I was busy processing what he and his friends have to do to take their shot at getting a piece of the pie when he added the clincher, the follow-up to the social worker's challenge to me so long ago: "Bein' Black," he said, "is a *hustle*."

The Difference Between Black and White College Graduates

And suddenly, I got it. Why they always laughed when I used the word, I mean.

See, I work hard. Everybody works hard. We really don't have a choice. Even hustling is hard, hard work because you have to stay on top of so many things at once and the pay-off is frequently disproportionately low and sometimes nonexistent. But the difference for *this* young man and most of the other young Black males in their senior year of college in 2006 in the United States is that, as *they* pass the major milestone of college graduation, a milestone that regularly puts *White* youths on the track to success immediately, *they're* still having to skulk around their neighborhoods in the dark, hedging their bets against an unsure future. Something I've never had to do before. And might well never have to do in my life. Even when I'm on welfare. It's all about options and, while Black may be beautiful ("Say it loud: I'm Black and proud!"), being Black is still a *serious* hustle.

A Longtime Recipient Looks at the Welfare System

Sugar Turner and Tracy Bachrach Ehlers

Sugar Turner is a school community outreach director and African American woman who was on welfare as a single mother for about seventeen years after her eighteenth birthday. Tracy Bachrach Ehlers is a cultural anthropologist and college professor at the University of Denver and an expert on women's and economic issues. Ehlers's other writings include Silent Looms: Women and Production in a Guatemalan Town.

Guiding coauthor Ehlers through a firsthand look at the local welfare office, Turner provides opinions on "don't-do-nothin'" recipients, on "hustlers" like herself who are determined to find a way to better their lives, on raising children without letting them stigmatize themselves over being on welfare, and on what would happen if welfare were discontinued. The welfare office visit that provided the background for the following selection took place in September 1995 or 1996, when the American welfare system was in transition.

Waiting time is stank. There's lots of people. All those welfare people are sitting around. Kids with dirty faces. Because you're poor, your kid's face doesn't have to be dirty. Unruly kids running around. Because you're poor, your kids don't have to be wild. And what's even more depressing is the number of men who are in there now. It used to be only women and children in the welfare office. And now there's men, and they appear to be able-bodied men, a lot of 'em. And they are there sitting right beside you in the welfare of-

Sugar Turner and Tracy Bachrach Ehlers, *Sugar's Life in the Hood: The Story of a Former Welfare Mother*, Austin, TX: University of Texas Press, 2002. Copyright © 2002 by Sugar Turner and Tracy Bachrach Ehlers. All rights reserved. Reproduced by permission of the University of Texas Press.

fice. There's no jobs. They may be drugged out. They may be alcoholed out. Whatever. They are disabled. So now they're relying on a check too.

If there were jobs in Springfield this man would not be there today. That didn't happen overnight to get him there. It's a process to get a man till he's so downtrodden, till he's so disabled that he's in the welfare office. He doesn't have one bad time and go "Well, I'm gonna go get on welfare." He still has the desire to want to provide for himself. And two, or three, or four bad times still don't kill that desire. But after you get kicked in the head more times than you can count, well . . .

Setting Oneself Apart

When I used to come here, I set myself apart. It's like I would go to the food-stamp office at a certain hour 'cause I didn't want to stand up in the line with all those welfare people lookin' hungry. I wouldn't *dare* go to the food-stamp office lookin' hungry. I don't want to be that needy. I don't want to be that dependent. I don't want anybody to think that I'm not gonna eat if I don't get food stamps. I'll make a way. I'll figure something out. I would not stand at that window and cry. If my kids are waiting for me outside in the car, I can't come out of there cryin', goin', "They wouldn't give me my food stamps." I can't do that. I'm a hustler. And I gotta figure out whatever it is I gotta do to get some food goin' on.

Inside yourself you feel embarrassed, because if you go to that window and you turn away with nothing, everybody knows somethin's wrong. Course they've all experienced it too, so everybody has the fear that if they go to the window, something could be wrong. You never know. The computer could be down, there could be a glitch, something could have happened to your paperwork. Each time you go up to their window, you're at their mercy. You can't call and ask, "Am I on the computer?" You have to go down and see. So you always have to present your face, and there's always the chance that your face could get egg on it.

The Staff Looks Worse than the Recipients

The workers at the Springfield Family Opportunity office are just sad. Anytime I went to see my technician, she'd never be dressed as good as me. Pills on her clothes. No jewelry. Nothing matching. I'd almost feel guilty. I'd turn my rings around. But of course, she probably drove, and I took the bus. And she probably has a life insurance policy for her kids, and I didn't have that. But on the surface, she never looked as happy as me. But look at her job! I feel sorry for her. She's dealing with welfare people every day. They're comin' in, dumpin' on you. So who's really poor? She's got all this baggage that's comin' in the door and it's her job. She's makin' $5 somethin', $6 somethin', $7 somethin' an hour to have people dump depression on her. I can't see that it would be worth it.

Technicians Are Human Too

Day in and day out you got people with sob stories. I respect 'em, and that's one of the reasons why I never gave them a hard time. They're human. They have feelings. So I think my experience with technicians was never terribly unpleasant because I was never terribly unpleasant. It all has to do with how you treat people and how you feel about yourself.

Also I knew that that's their job. And I realized that it didn't have anything to do with me. . . . So I never took any of that away with me.

You can have the butt-ugliest woman for a technician. Good Lord in the morning Jesus, her figure is horrible! She's totally unhealthy. Or you can have someone ugly as a mud fence but who you can tell loves themselves, cares about themself. She obviously doesn't. . . .

Being a Hustler

You don't want to be no welfare bitch—which is just an ignorant, loud-mouth, collect-a-check, don't-do-nothin', don't-comb-her-hair, don't-keep-her-kids, just-don't-care-who-knows-her-business type of broad. That's who she is. You can talk about welfare with other women, but you don't tell your business out loud in a parking lot! There's a certain protocol.

No way would I do that. I'm a hustler, and I have faith that the Lord is going to make a way for me. And my faith is not in man. So if the office is closed, I'm cool. If I'm standing at that window and they're telling me my food stamps aren't there, and they really aren't there, then maybe there's a lesson in there for me. Maybe there's a reason why my food stamps aren't there. My faith is in the Lord. I'm goin' to eat. I don't know what I'm gonna do, but I'm goin' to eat. I'm gonna pawn my rings. I'll go over to Grandma's. There's any number of people I can call. These aren't people I could say, give me a thousand dollars, but a meal, *that* I could ask for. There's no way I could look my kids in the face and say we not eatin'.

Keeping It from the Kids

And I'd never bring my kids to the welfare office. Because kids don't need to see it. They don't need to grow up knowing that welfare is their daddy. Kids can grow up and not know they're on welfare if you try hard. But you can't deny it bringin' 'em into the office.

It's like if their daddy's in jail. You don't take them into the jail because then they get a whole sense of it, a feel, a smell. As long as it's just in their mind, they don't have nothin' to really attach it to. You bring 'em to the welfare office with those unhappy people waitin' around all day, then they know what welfare is. It makes a mentality that they don't need to have. It's a handicap. Because then they know that they're different than other kids.

Repealin' welfare means you gonna find more newborn kids in trash cans. You're gonna find more crime, more drugs, more violence. People are gonna be frustrated. It shouldn't be this way, but sometimes welfare is people's only hope. If you're struggling for the month, sometimes your only hope is that the first is coming. That might be the only thing that keeps you from killing these kids, beatin' 'em, throwing yourself over a bridge, droppin' 'em out this window. If you can just hold out till the first and you get your check. On the first, you feel better and they feel better, and you can hold out till the next first of the month. It lends some hope.

Motherhood Is as Valuable as Employment

If the government takes away their checks, welfare mothers will be up the creek. It'll be a struggle. Every day they'll feel like shit. They wouldn't start robbin' banks or whatever, but their lives would be even more dilapidated. The only jobs they could get would be just like welfare, only worse. You can't tell somebody that they're gonna get some positive feelings sweeping sidewalks for forty hours, and they're supposed to feel some satisfaction about going to work to earn your food stamps and your check. They're gonna be a mean, disgruntled bunch of bitches. Ain't nobody gonna be able to stand 'em. They're not gonna have any purpose. At least if you're on welfare, you have the purpose of staying home, taking care of your kids, keeping the cleanest house on the block, being able to go to maybe some PTA meetings, and everything.

And now, the government's beatin' you up for doin' it, and for valuin' being a mother. If you take that away and you say, sweep sidewalks all day for this funky-ass check, there'd be a whole class of really mean people with nothin'. No dream, no nothin'.

The Problems with Reformed Welfare

Karen Seccombe

Karen Seccombe is a professor of sociology at Portland State University. She has written or coauthored numerous articles and book chapters on women's and family issues, aging, poverty, and welfare. Most of the welfare recipients interviewed for her book So You Think I Drive a Cadillac?, *from which the following selection is excerpted, were single mothers who came from a variety of racial and family backgrounds.*

The five single mothers on welfare comment on their problems with a system they still find "frustrating, demoralizing, and in need of considerable change" since the reforms of 1996. The most common complaints are that benefits are still inadequate to provide even a minimal standard of decent living, the system is impersonal and insensitive, and fulfilling the system's work requirements actually leaves a woman worse off financially.

Many women lament that the welfare system provides benefits at such a low level, that it is virtually impossible to maintain a decent standard of living for their children. An AFDC [Aid to Families with Dependent Children] grant in the region where the interviews were conducted was $241 dollars a month for a parent with one child, $303, $364, and $426 for a parent with two, three, and four children, respectively, where it remains in 2005. In other words, the check did not increase between 1996 and 2005 despite a significant rise in the cost of living.

Karen Seccombe, *So You Think I Drive a Cadillac?: Welfare Recipients' Perspectives on the System and Its Reform*, 2nd edition. Published by Allyn & Bacon, Boston, MA. Copyright © 2007 by Pearson Education. Reprinted by permission of the publisher.

Welfare Recipients and Applicants

Jasmine: "Just Don't Have Enough Money"

Jasmine, a 35-year-old African American mother of two children is employed part-time, but continues to receive a partial welfare benefit because of her low earnings. She would prefer to work full-time, as she has done in the past, but when her two children began having severe asthma attacks, she cut back her hours so that she could take care of them. She told me that she feels uncomfortable leaving them with a babysitter. Luckily, she has relatives who can watch them during her reduced work hours; they are knowledgeable about asthma, and how to treat it, in case an attack were to occur. Like others, Jasmine is frustrated by the size of her welfare grant and her reduction in food stamps, believing that they are inadequate for taking care of children:

> I simply don't get enough food stamps. And the cash . . . are you kidding? They keep asking me, "How are you paying your rent, how are you paying your rent?" It's like, hey, if you'd give me more money, I could answer that. And she's like, "But this doesn't add up. Your income and your outcome don't add up. You just don't have enough money." And I'm like, why do you think I'm here? Yes, I don't have enough money. They are implying . . . what? That I'm selling my body, or what? You know? I bounce checks, there's your answer.

Stephanie: "How Can Anyone Grow Up Normal Living Like That?"

Stephanie expressed anger that a country as wealthy as ours spends so little to take care of its children. She began this conversation with a discussion of substandard housing that low-income people may reside in:

> Is something going to come out and bite me? This is the equivalent of the Black Plague, with all the rats. How can anyone grow up normal, intelligent, and become a productive member of society living like that? I don't understand.

And when you're hungry at night, or when your child goes to bed cold, how can you expect them to go to school the next morning and learn anything? You know, [psychologist Abraham] Maslow's hierarchy of needs. If you don't meet the very bottom ones, how are you supposed to be anything on top? We're humans, and will resort to survival skills. And I'm sure that's what many people are doing. Just surviving. I've known a lot of women who live in these villages [student family housing at the university] who are not as fortunate as I am. I mean, I had a house full of stuff when I moved in here because I already had a house. I mean, how can any child grow up and be stimulated in an environment where they may or may not be able to heat the house, or be able to afford the extra 20 or 30 dollars that I hand over at the end of the month to buy food? Or they may not be able to go out and buy the clothing that their child needs when they outgrow it, or the shoes. Most of the time I can swing it. But, like I said, if it wasn't for family housing and living on campus, and my financial aid, there would be no way.

Not Just Whining

When mothers on welfare complain about the amount of money they receive, they are not just whining for the sake of it. Children who are deprived of adequate financial support suffer long-term consequences. [Sociologists Sara] McLanahan and [Gary] Sandefur, in their award winning book, *Growing Up with a Single Parent* (1994), report that income is a significant factor, although certainly not the only one, in explaining the deleterious effects of growing up in a single-parent household. Using several data sources from nationally representative samples across the United States, they found that children in single-parent households are less likely to graduate from high school; they are less likely to enroll in and graduate from college; they are more likely to be out of work; and girls are more likely to become teen mothers than are those children who have grown up in two-parent households. Income itself accounts for approximately half of the differences between the two groups. Thus, our government's tradition of supporting children inadequately has serious long-term consequences.

A second concern with the welfare system was over the way in which services were delivered. Women repeatedly described many problems: They complained that the system is far too impersonal; caseworkers are unhelpful; the push is on to find a job, any job, regardless of the quality of it; there should be more one-on-one help; child support payments should be more closely enforced and monitored; and the delivery of medical services through the Public Health Unit were problematic. Moreover, women repeatedly told me that the system is cumbersome and complicated.

Alexandra: "Nobody Is There to Help You"

Alexandra, a 29-year-old white woman who has been on welfare for four years, describes the maze she encountered when she lost her job and turned to welfare for help:

> I mean, when you start on welfare, you have to start depending on people that are already on welfare to get you into the system because nobody is there to help you, and there are no guidelines to go by to tell you how. I just needed some assistance at the time, and I wanted to go back to school and stuff, but I couldn't get assistance because I couldn't figure out how. I kept going down for appointments, and I couldn't get in there. It's just like you have to know somebody to be able to get on it and get through it. It's like a maze; it's like a puzzle, and you have to fit the pieces together, and you have to start learning how to work the system, basically. It's like a job learning how to do it, and I was real naïve. I never saw a food stamp in my life. I never saw a WIC [Women, Infants, and Children] check, you know. I didn't even know what an AFDC check looked like. I had never even known a person who used them.

Becky: "Stop and Look at the Individual"

Becky, a 23-year-old white woman who works nearly full-time cleaning houses, summarized the concerns of many when she complained that services are delivered without individuals' needs in mind. If people are on welfare because of varying circumstances, then their needs are likely to differ as well. They may need different things in order to help them get *off* welfare.

> There needs to be more individual one-on-one help. Meet the individual's need, instead of forcing them to conform to some generic lot and saying take it or leave it. I feel like a hypocrite being on AFDC because I don't agree with it and its way of treating people. It treats everybody the same, but it needs to stop and look at the individual and try to help each individual person according to what they need. No patch solutions.

The third weakness of the welfare system that was repeatedly emphasized is that welfare benefits are significantly reduced or eliminated prematurely when a recipient acquires a job. Given the options of low-paying work for welfare recipients, their incomes are not sufficient to pull them out of poverty. Moreover, when working, they face a new host of challenges and difficulties, such as needing transportation, childcare, or requiring additional clothing or frequent laundering of uniforms. Many women would be willing to take on these extra challenges, but with their cash grant, food stamps, housing subsidies, and Medicaid cut, they are in a worse financial predicament than they were while they were home receiving welfare. Is it worth it, they ask themselves? . . .

Dee: "Just Enough Money to Keep You Going"

No woman interviewed was opposed to reforming the welfare system because all recognized that it does little to improve life circumstances. Dee questions whether welfare, even in the aftermath of reform, even tries to help women.

> They give you just enough money to keep you going with helping with rent and the utility bill, just enough to keep you going and looking forward to that next month's check. So therefore, you look forward to next month's check. In a sense, they baited the hook and you done took a bite out of it, and now they are fighting you there.

SOCIAL ISSUES FIRSTHAND

CHAPTER 2

Other Perspectives on Welfare

Working in Human Services Is Rewarding

Ana Pagan

Ana Pagan, director of the Merced County Human Services Agency in California and 2007 president of the National Staff Development and Training Association (an affiliate of the American Public Human Services Association), has introduced various innovations into welfare programs.

In the following article, Pagan discusses the challenges and rewards of her more than twenty-five years helping "hardworking people with limited resources" deal with bureaucracy and become self-sufficient. She admits disliking the term welfare, *considering* human services *more accurate and less demeaning. Anyone—not only specific categories of people—can become temporarily disadvantaged, says Pagan, and providing assistance is everyone's duty.*

I have worked for 14 years for public human service agencies. Before that, I worked for 12 years in agricultural human resources. Meeting the needs of farm laborers involved field social work. Housing, health care, legal issues—I helped hardworking people with limited resources deal with them all.

From the Private to the Public Sector

Rewards of the job: My move from the private sector to the public sector was intentional. The drive to make the world a better place is what brings people to human services. In human services, like teaching, the motivation is to mine the good stuff in human beings and bring it forward.

[Recently] a young man walked up to me in a store. He asked, "Ana Pagan? You might not remember me because I

Ana Pagan, "Our Do'ers Profile," *Policy & Practice*, vol. 64, June 2006, p. 44. Reproduced by permission.

was 8 years old the last time you saw me. I have always wondered what happened to you and hoped one day I could thank you. You really saved my life. Because of your work with my parents, I was encouraged to go to school, earned a degree, and I have a wife and child. My life is good."

I cannot begin to tell you what an incredible feeling it was to hear him say I had been important in his life.

Introducing Innovations in Welfare

Accomplishments Most Proud of: When it was clear in the early 1990s that welfare reform was coming, I started a program to train welfare recipients to become licensed childcare providers and engaged the business community to help us move people to work. More recently, I have positioned a medium-sized Central California county to be an innovator in human services. Merced County has been a leader in bringing back integrated services, improving accuracy rates, bringing law enforcement on staff, and working with the animal shelter on the link between animal abuse, domestic violence, elder abuse, and child maltreatment.

I am proud of the fact that I am ... president of the National Staff Development and Training Association [an affiliate of the American Public Human Services Association]. It is an honor to work with professionals who give so much of themselves to bring along the next generation of workers.

Personal: In my youth, I had the life-altering experience of knowing Sarah T. Gold. She was my teacher. She helped mold my social consciousness, awakened in me a love of learning and sparked my curiosity about life and people. It was from her that I absorbed the desire to teach. I am a teacher and a trainer at heart.

Future Challenges for the Delivery of Public Services: Finding ways to work prevention into existing programs. In Merced, we integrate all services as a philosophy. We are redefining our Food Stamp Program as part of our effort to address the increase in obesity and diabetes. At intake, we encourage all women to get a mammogram. We have had women come back and tell us that their breast cancer was caught early, giving them a better chance at recovery.

Redefining "Welfare"

I would like to eradicate the word *welfare* because people think that our services are only for the poor. I would like to redefine the work we do in the minds of the community as a social safety net that anyone may need at any given time. Realistically, most people are one catastrophe away from needing some kind of assistance. The biggest challenge for the future is to elevate the understanding that we all benefit if we help our neighbor. Pay now or pay later; it is so much more cost-effective to prevent things from happening.

Investigating How the New Welfare Works

Sharon Hays

Sharon Hays, a former social worker and later a sociology professor at the University of Virginia, is currently a professor of sociology and gender studies at the University of Southern California. Her books include Flat Broke with Children: Women in the Age of Welfare Reform *and* The Cultural Contradictions of Motherhood.

In the article that follows, the author describes her experiences conducting three years of extensive research on the new welfare system of 1996 and its effects. After interviewing numerous recipients and caseworkers and observing firsthand the procedures involved, she concludes that while current welfare laws have certain advantages—such as increased benefits for low-income mothers—the new system is not nearly as successful as its proponents claim. Significant reforms are still necessary, she contends, to ensure that all Americans earn income proportionate to their willingness to work and that they have access to affordable, good-quality child care and housing.

It was a lot tougher than I expected it to be, studying welfare reform. I knew I had to examine the impact of the 1996 Personal Responsibility Act. I had listened closely to the politicians as they hammered out the language and logic of this law. I analyzed the newly established work rules. I read carefully the law's condemnation of single parenting. I pondered the larger social significance of removing the 61-year-old guarantee of a safety net for the nation's most desperately poor

Sharon Hays, "Studying the Quagmire of Welfare Reform," *The Chronicle of Higher Education*, vol. 50, October 17, 2003, p. B7. Copyright © 2003 by The Chronicle of Higher Education. This article may not be published, reposted, or redistributed without express permission from The Chronicle.

women and children. And I tried to take seriously the Congressional proclamation that welfare reform would "end the dependence of needy parents on government benefits by promoting job preparation, work, and marriage."

I was skeptical. All that was needed, this law seemed to be saying, was to educate the poor in "mainstream" American values of work and family life. But I had to wonder, were welfare recipients really just suffering from bad values? Did they need new ones? Would they find them in the welfare office?

Preparing to See Welfare Firsthand

In any case, it was apparent to me that the majority of Congressional policy makers had never spent much time in the world of welfare; never followed the routines of a welfare office; never lived in ghetto poverty; never raised a child without the help of nannies, au pairs, housekeepers, or (at least) the best in child-care centers; never spent a month trying to make ends meet on a $350 welfare check. But then again, neither had I. To make sense of this law, to see how it would all unfold, I wanted to be inside the welfare office.

I thought I was well prepared for the task. As a scholar of gender, work, and family life, and a theorist of American culture, I felt confidently armed with the proper intellectual tools. And having spent my first years out of college as a street-level social worker, I figured that the structure of the welfare office would hold few surprises, and I was sure that I knew how to handle myself in poor neighborhoods. After all, in those younger days I'd spent time with drug addicts, murderers, and thieves; I'd worked with people who abused their kids, visited heroin-shooting galleries, and watched dogfights staged on the street for the sake of gambling and sport. Nothing in the world of welfare could rattle me.

Or so I thought.

Three Years Visiting Welfare Offices and Recipients

To write my book, *Flat Broke with Children: Women in the Age of Welfare Reform*, I spent three years, from December 1997 to January 2001, visiting welfare offices and the homes of welfare families. Most of my time was spent in and around two welfare offices—one in a medium-size town in the Southeast I call Arbordale, another in a large metropolitan area in the West that I call Sunbelt City. I interviewed clients and caseworkers, hung out in waiting rooms, attended all the training sessions and caseworker meetings that welfare recipients are required to attend, went through all the forms they have to fill out. I visited the homes of welfare mothers and talked to them there. I spent a lot of time in housing projects.

Stepping into the Crossfire of the Welfare Debate

In researching poverty and the welfare system, I knew I was entering the ranks of hundreds of scholars who had taken up these issues before me. Yet my ethnographic approach was crucial, I thought, in providing an angle of vision that was missing in all the statistical accountings, policy analyses, and philosophical renderings that make up the bulk of research on welfare. At the same time, in my theoretical approach to studying reform, I took up a position in the crossfire of a long-standing scholarly debate. While conservative scholars have consistently argued that the problems of welfare stem from the bad values of welfare recipients and the bad values promoted by the old welfare system, liberals have long countered that the problems of welfare are primarily problems of economic inequality. Risking the ire of both sides, I set out to systematically examine the question of values, but in this case I aimed to uncover both the good and the bad in the values of welfare clientele and in the values of the newly reformed welfare system.

An Overwhelming Number of Complicating Factors

It didn't take a genius to figure out that there would be a vast difference between policy makers' lofty goals and the more complex realities of life in the welfare office. What I wasn't prepared for was the sheer number of complicating factors—the layers of contradiction, the multiplicity of experiences and outcomes, the depth of hardship, the height of public affirmation, and the daunting range of interests, ideals, and misconceptions that shaped interpretations of just what was at stake. More than once in the course of my research I found myself wondering why I hadn't picked a simpler, less painful, and less controversial topic. I wistfully imagined how comfortable it might have been to study the dating practices of my college students or the consumption habits of my middle-class friends.

From the moment I set foot in the welfare office, I knew I had entered a quagmire. By early 1998, the White House was already applauding the results of reform, and the nightly news was already offering "human interest" coverage of smiling former welfare mothers gainfully employed in local supermarkets and small businesses. But the welfare caseworkers and clients I met were a good deal less sanguine. Caseworkers in Arbordale and Sunbelt City were still frantically trying to decipher all the rules and regulations of reform, still worried about whether they'd be able to keep up with the federal demand that they place an ever-increasing proportion of their clients in jobs, still spending their lunch breaks complaining about multiple glitches in the new computer systems, and still wondering whether they'd be able to convince their clients that the newly instituted lifetime limits on welfare benefits were both absolute and here to stay.

Understanding the Typical Welfare Client

Welfare clients, for their part, noticed immediately that something big was happening. And, like caseworkers, they were struggling to determine just what the nation was asking of them, and wondering if they'd be able to manage. To understand the experience of welfare clients, and to make sense of their responses, it's important to know what I now know about this group of Americans. The vast majority of adult welfare recipients—over 90 percent—are mothers. Nearly all are raising their children alone. Over 80 percent have work experience, but more than half are without high school diplomas, and nearly as many suffer from physical or mental-health disabilities that affect their ability to work. National studies suggest that about half have been the victims of domestic violence or sexual abuse. And welfare mothers have, on average, two children to worry about when they consider the costs and benefits of the jobs available to them.

The primary message these women heard when they arrived at the newly reformed Arbordale and Sunbelt City welfare offices was simple—you must get a job, get it fast, and accept whatever wages or hours you can get. The pressure was intense. It began with the mandatory "job search" requiring 40 verifiable job contacts in 30 days and the employability and skills assessments and the three- to five-day "job readiness" workshops that offered tips on how to dress for an interview, balance one's budget, manage child-care arrangements, cope with stress, and speak proper English rather than street slang.

Employment Training for Low-Wage Jobs

Most of the welfare mothers who hadn't found a job within the first 30 days were placed in full-time employment-training programs. In Arbordale and Sunbelt City, nearly all these training programs were geared to low-wage jobs: nursing assistants, cook's helpers, introductory computer skills, child care, and janitorial work. Those welfare clients who were still unemployed at the completion of training, or those for whom training was deemed inappropriate, were assigned an unpaid "workfare" placement—sweeping city streets, serving food at school cafeterias, sorting papers for a county agency—working at least 30 hours a week in return for their welfare checks. Throughout, all welfare mothers were required to meet regularly with their welfare caseworkers to report on their overall progress toward "self-sufficiency."

While welfare mothers were spending 30 to 40 hours a week in all those seminars, training programs, and workfare placements, they also had to find some place to put their kids. If they were lucky, well organized, flexible, patient, and persistent, they could hope to be among the less than one-third of all welfare mothers who actually receive the federal child-care subsidies for which all poor families are technically eligible. If they were not so lucky, they'd have to somehow, manage child care on their $350-a-month (average) welfare income.

"Sanctioned" by the Welfare System

Inside the welfare office, the demanding, lock-step work requirements of reform were enforced not just through the time limits on benefits, but also through the system of "sanctions." Welfare mothers who failed to attend job-readiness or employment-training sessions, failed to make a sufficient number of job contacts, failed to follow through on a workfare placement, or failed to report changes in their employment circumstances were sanctioned. These sanctioned welfare clients lost all or part of their family's welfare check for a specified number of months—they lost, in other words, their primary source of income. Nationwide, sanction rates have more than doubled since reform.

As one might guess, many of the poor mothers I met came to call this new welfare system the "work rigamarole." Many considered the use of sanctions inhumane, some referred to the workfare programs as a new form of "slavery," a good number complained bitterly of difficulties with child care, and many of the repeat customers recalled nostalgically those earlier days when the welfare office "was a whole lot more peaceful."

Exhausting Just to Watch

I couldn't help but agree. I found myself exhausted just watching this process. And by 2001 most of the caseworkers I knew were exhausted as well. A number of them had quit their jobs.

I knew full well that the best way to sell a book was to have a simple and straightforward message, cleanly packaged, preferably summed up in a single phrase and punctuated with an exclamation point. If I'd stopped at this point in the tale of reform, and added a rendering of the many individual horror stories that accompanied it, I'd be able to wrap it all up quite neatly. Unfortunately, by the time I understood this part of the story, I also knew that there was another side to this tale, and a number of different ways to read it.

At the same time that welfare reform instituted a whole new set of impossibly demanding and often punitive rules, it also brought with it a smaller, but significant, set of positive "supportive services." Those services included not just that (grossly insufficient) assistance in paying for child care, but also help in covering the cost of transportation, clothing, and supplies for work and, in special cases, aid in covering expenses like rent and utility payments, repairing one's car, purchasing eyeglasses, and paying for dental work. Welfare reform also allowed those mothers whose earnings from work were very low to continue to receive welfare benefits. This support was limited, and all of it was tied to the work requirements. Nonetheless, most of the welfare mothers I met were grateful for this assistance.

Most Welfare Clients Do Support Personal Responsibility

Further clouding my darker portrait of reform was the stunning fact that the majority of welfare mothers I met actually liked welfare reform. That is, even though many welfare clients disliked (or abhorred) the endless stream of rules and regulations that came with this law, most remained in favor of the Personal Responsibility Act. They wanted to work, they wanted their children to see them working, they wanted to be free of the welfare office, and they wanted financial independence.

Confusing matters even further, the more I talked to my colleagues, friends, and neighbors about my research, the more it became clear to me that everyone had his or her own agenda when it came to interpreting the significance of welfare reform. It was about poverty. It was about race. It was about women and motherhood. It was about work. It was about cutting costs. Some of my colleagues thought that international comparisons of state welfare policies were the only worthy approach to analyzing the significance of reform. Others thought the most important factor in assessing the Personal Responsibility Act was the racial discrimination that lies behind its more punitive and unforgiving features. A good number of my neighbors, on the other hand, remained convinced that welfare mothers were morally "undeserving"—lazy, promiscuous, and prone to illegal behavior and abuse of the system. These women, they said, needed to be taught a lesson.

I was dizzy.

Was Welfare Reform Really a Success?

Before I could regain my balance, I was faced with the "success" of welfare reform. By the time I was completing my research, the American public had been so frequently assured that the goals of reform had been met that they had turned their attention elsewhere. The welfare rolls had been cut by more than half (from 12 million recipients in 1996 to 5 million in 2002), and most former welfare mothers were employed. So it seemed that, even if there were still problems with the system, and even if there were still questions left unanswered about work, family, race, poverty, motherhood, and morality, wasn't it true that the Personal Responsibility Act had done its job? Wasn't it time to celebrate?

From where I sat, there were still plenty of things to worry about. Just as there was a vast difference between policy makers' goals and the more disturbing realities I saw inside the welfare office, there was also a wide gap between the political celebrations of the success of welfare reform and the hardship I encountered. And if you read the statistics carefully, you could see that. By 2002, nearly half (40 percent) of the women and children who had left the welfare rolls had no discernible source of income—no work, no welfare, nowhere to go. Of the 60 percent of former welfare recipients who were employed, half were still living in poverty. Their average annual earnings were estimated at $8,000 to $10,000 a year, and most had jobs without medical insurance, sick leave, or retirement benefits.

Off Welfare but Still in Poverty

Thus, in the context of the then-booming economy, more than two-thirds of the women and children who had left the welfare office as a result of reform were still living well below the poverty level. Although the welfare rolls had been cut by more than half, the number of families living in dire (welfare-level) poverty had declined by only 15 percent. What this meant, and what I knew to be true, was that millions of poor families were now more reluctant than ever to seek out help from the welfare office. State governments and local charities were already reporting rising rates of hunger and homelessness. And the economy had begun to sour.

As I read those numbers, I could not forget that they were referring to real people, to mothers and children. I also could not forget that there were millions of poor families still on the welfare rolls. New ones were coming in each day, others were coming back again. I knew all the stories about problems in managing the graveyard shift, what it was like to find child care when one of the kids was sick, what it meant to have the phone turned off, how it felt to be unable to afford birthday gifts or winter coats, the major difficulties caused by flat tires or buses that didn't run on schedule, the distress of women forced to leave their children at home alone, the overdue power bills, the slum landlords, the problems with depression and stress.

Welfare Is Failing Families

In the end, it was clear to me that, although the outcomes of welfare reform would emerge slowly, and although there were a good number of real success stories among the millions who had left the rolls, in the long run this law would not only result in rising rates of hunger and homelessness, but also rising rates of crime; rising numbers of women in mental-health facilities and domestic-violence shelters; rising numbers of children in foster care, in substandard child care, or left to fend for themselves; and rising numbers of working-poor families stretched to the breaking point.

All of this brought me to the final disorienting confusion that I encountered in writing this book. It was my damn bleeding heart. Believe me, most of the time I don't fit anybody's image of a "typical" bleeding heart. Yet in this context, my deeply buried Mother-Teresa tendencies emerged. It was all I could do to avoid the impulse to shelter and shield many of the desperately poor families I encountered, especially the children. But by the time I completed my research, I also knew that my pity was ultimately as demeaning and degrading to welfare families as the relentless rules and regulations of the welfare system.

It slowly dawned on me that it was that curious paradox I'd found in the welfare office that held the key to unpacking both the problems and promise of welfare reform. It was the fact that, as much as most welfare mothers disliked reform, the majority still believed that the new system was better than the old. The more I listened to welfare recipients, the more I came to recognize the tremendous cultural power of the ideal of welfare reform—that no one should be "dependent" on welfare, that all Americans should be able to support themselves and their children.

Looking at the results of reform, I also saw that worthy ideals and good values were not enough. To make those good intentions a reality, what was needed were decent jobs that paid a family wage, serious education and training programs that offered access to real career ladders, guarantees of quality child care, affordable housing, and reliable medical coverage. What was needed were programs that included poor men as well as women, and included the working poor as well as the nonworking poor. What was needed, in short, was a real commitment to the "mainstream" American values that the Personal Responsibility Act had claimed to champion.

One of the Most Important Issues of Our Time

In thinking about this, I also came to recognize that all the seemingly disparate agendas of my friends, neighbors, and colleagues were on target, at least to some extent. Welfare reform is simultaneously about work, family, poverty, race, capitalism, motherhood, and morality. It is about problems of gender and race inequality, the widening gap between rich and poor, widespread difficulties in juggling work and family commitments, and the significant question of how this nation will respond to its most disadvantaged members....

All those concerns seem even more pressing to me now. And I am absolutely convinced that welfare reform, in all its complexity and with all the proclamations of its "success," remains one of the most urgent and important issues of our time.

Welfare and Child Care

Gina Adams

Gina Adams is a senior research associate at the Urban Institute, a nonpartisan organization dedicated to promoting reform and educated debate regarding public policy. Adams, director of child-care and early-education research at the institute's Center on Labor, Human Services, and Population, was codirector (with Pamela Holcomb) of a recent extensive study on child-care subsidies and the Temporary Assistance to Needy Families (TANF) program.

In the following article, Adams looks at five questions regarding child-care subsidies and the welfare-to-work system: Why are subsidies so important? Are the programs really compatible? What are state and local agencies doing? Is high quality in child care a major goal of the subsidy system? What research is the Urban Institute currently conducting on child care? While generally optimistic, her answers recognize the need for further work to ensure balanced priorities, implementation of new ideas, and high-quality care that fosters the mental and social development of young children.

1. Why are child care subsidies so crucial for welfare-to-work parents?

Most parents on welfare must work or attend training to receive welfare. It would be impossible for them to do that, and be a responsible parent, if they didn't have someone to take care of their children. Subsidies help them afford child care, which can be both expensive and hard to find.

Gina Adams, "Five Questions for Gina Adams," *Urban Institute*, April 6, 2006. Reproduced by permission. www.urban.org/toolkit/fivequestions/GAdams.cfm.

Balancing Work Requirements and Parental Responsibilities

Child care subsidies are designed to make sure that parents don't have to choose between meeting their work requirements and being a good parent. Subsidies are more important than ever since 1996 when time limits were put on welfare. Time limits pressure parents to get into the workforce quickly. Finding affordable care for their children in such a short time frame can be the biggest hurdle.

These issues are even more pressing now, given that the most recent TANF reauthorization requires states to put a significantly higher proportion of their welfare cases into jobs and work-related activities.

2. Do the child care and welfare systems work well together?

Actually, three systems must work together to help a family moving from welfare to work get child care—the cash assistance system, the employment and training system, and the child care subsidy system. Each system is very devolved, so the melding can vary greatly by place.

A team of UI [Urban Institute] researchers, which [child-development and labor-market expert] Pamela Holcomb and I co-directed, just finished a study funded by the [U.S. Department of Health and Human Services] Child Care Bureau that looked at 11 sites across the country to see how they were coordinating systems. We found enormous variation in how much parents had to do, whether the systems were in one agency or multiple agencies, how the caseworkers were involved, and who was responsible for doing what to ensure the family gets the subsidy.

It's the End Result That Counts

Interestingly, there wasn't a lot of connection between the system's administrative complexity and what parents had to do. Parents cared only about the end result. Some localities may have three agencies involved, but parents have only to go

Other Perspectives on Welfare

one place and meet with one caseworker. Others might only have one agency, but the parents get shuffled among several different caseworkers.

There's no easy way to say whether any particular site did it right. Instead, we found some promising practices, as well as problematic ones, in many sites. On the promising side were attempts to simplify the process for parents. For instance, by giving more child care responsibilities to the welfare-to-work caseworker, or by setting it up so that parents have to work with only one worker who can manage the communication among the different systems.

But we also found conflicting priorities. For example, on the welfare-to-work side is the drive to get the parent into a work activity as soon as possible. The time limit clock is ticking. For families who already have found child care, that's no problem. For families that don't have child care, it can take time to find good care. Often, good child care programs have waiting lists.

Giving Parents Time to Find Child Care

So one important question is whether agencies give parents enough time to find the right child care. Agencies require families to start the work activities from a few days to two weeks after they apply for welfare, though will extend the deadline if parents can't find child care. Agencies we talked to felt that this approach worked well.

But talking with parents gave us a somewhat different message. Many parents talked about needing more time and help finding care. Although they find some place to put their children, it isn't clear that they've made the choices they want—which isn't good for anyone.

Another challenging area is that having a subsidy can—in some cases—be very tightly tied to a work activity or a job. Yet, work activities are often short-term and have gaps, and parents can lose their jobs—which means that the subsidy can

Welfare

be very unstable. A study in five states found that the average child care subsidy spell was 3 to 7 months. This is a problem for parents, agencies, and children because we know that kids need long-term stable relationships with caring adults.

3. What are some innovative state and local child care practices?

We have another study currently under way that looks at how state and local child care subsidy agencies can make it easier for parents to get and keep subsidies. A number of states are identifying ways to do this. For example, our earlier work found that many states required parents to report every change in their circumstances—such as a change in job, schedule, or pay—to make sure that the subsidy was at the right level. Yet, such precision creates burdens both administratively and for parents.

Experimenting with Flexibility

Our study finds that some states are experimenting with ways to be more flexible. Examples include finding alternative ways for parents to report changes, minimizing the kinds of changes they have to report, and not changing the subsidy unless the change is significant.

Simplifying the application form, using the same applications in all programs (such as food stamps and child care), and connecting data systems so that parents have to report changes to only one system are also being tried. So if a family reports an employment change to the employment system, the information gets sent to the child care system. Sharing data can be a win-win for everyone.

Not all good practices are complicated or expensive—and they can be easy for other states to adopt. My favorite example is putting the parent's recertification date on the bottom of attendance forms sent to providers. This allows the provider to work with the parent to make sure they recertify. It doesn't cost anything.

Often, the poorest localities can do amazing things through leadership and vision of the local agency management. One of the sites we visited consistently made parent-provider service top priority. Those workers would stay up all night to get those checks out on time if they had to. And when you talked with parents and providers in that site, you could tell that the program worked fairly well for them. This is in a state with relatively few resources.

What Works in Theory Does Not Always Work in Practice

Yet, sometimes, on paper it looks like a state has done something very innovative that we realize when we visit isn't working at all. For example, in theory, a family is supposed to be able to do all of their reporting by phone. But then we find out the agencies don't have enough people to answer the phones.

4. Is quality a goal of the child care subsidy system?

Yes and no. A small portion of the Child Care and Development Fund—which is the primary source of federal funding for child care—goes to help improve quality of child care overall. And a number of states contribute additional funds above that level. But it's too few dollars to influence the entire child care market. Most child care funds go out through subsidy vouchers designed to help families afford the child care that is already available. They're not designed to change the child care market itself.

Clearly, many state and local administrators in the country are working hard to figure out how to spend those dollars effectively to improve things for kids. Some states are experimenting with paying higher rates for higher quality care—which can be a promising strategy as long as states pay enough to really support quality. But it's difficult. Many states haven't raised their basic pay rates in years. The maximum amount that they'll pay doesn't cover a good range of the higher-charging providers.

More Child Care or Better Child Care?

States are in a quandary—pay more for better services and subsidize fewer families or hold rates steady and take more families off the waiting list? This is a very real trade-off for them since funding in recent years has stagnated and, recently, has started decreasing in some states.

5. What else is the [Urban Institute's] child care [research] team working on?

One of our most exciting projects is our study of child care providers and the child care subsidy system in five counties across the country. Such a study is long overdue since remarkably little is known about the child care providers upon whom the subsidy system depends—the last national study of child care providers was in 1990. We're examining who does and doesn't participate in the subsidy system and assessing whether they differ on some key indicators of quality. We are also looking at how various policies and practices affect providers.

One of the issues we are most interested in is exploring how our research results may spawn ideas about designing subsidies to support quality. For example, it allows us to think about how to design and frame policies to help bolster the parts of the system that aren't meeting the needs of children and families.

Differences Between Racial and Ethnic Groups

We also just released a study examining child care patterns by race and ethnicity. It warns policymakers and program administrators not to assume that national patterns hold true for any particular group. Our findings do show that non-parental care is a huge issue for all groups. Eighty percent or more of children younger than five with working parents are in non-parental care. But the kind of care varies. Black children are much more likely to be in centers. Hispanic children are the least likely to be in centers and the most likely to be in a relative's care.

What all this points out is that we really need to be thinking about how we can best support quality care in *every* setting. It is such a critical issue—I am often worried that the policy debate about school readiness and preparing children for school is focused too narrowly on developing prekindergarten programs for 4 year olds. While this is an exciting and important strategy, we can't afford to forget that the larger child care market, and the subsidy system serves millions of low-income children each day, and many of them are spending significant time in these settings.

If we don't *also* focus on how to support quality there—for the infants and toddlers whose brains are developing and who are getting that critical early foundation for future learning, for 3–4 year olds whose parents work full-time and who may not be able to use a part-day part-year preschool program, and for the school-age children whose after-school time is critical for their school success—then we can't ensure that all of our children will succeed.

Waiting at a Welfare Office

Karen Wilhelm

The volunteer process for tutoring at a girls' residential facility brought Karen Wilhelm to a Family Independence (welfare) Agency where a routine background check quickly turned into a maze of delays, technicalities, and vagaries. The following essay describes how Wilhelm not only came to wonder how many potential volunteers gave up before being approved, but observed firsthand the frustrations endured by welfare applicants and recipients in the "human inventory holding area." Wilhelm is a professional researcher, consultant, and editor from Detroit.

I doubt that many of us visit the welfare office very often. I ventured into one yesterday—not down on my luck, fortunately, but on a different waste of time. I told myself I'd learn something, and I did.

First, why did I go? I am applying to be a volunteer tutor at a residential facility for girls whose families can't care for them, nor can they fit into the foster care system. It's imperative to protect the girls, and volunteers have to jump through several hoops, one of which is a background check of some kind. This is done at the Family Independence Agency, which in Michigan means "We'll give you some money, but get off your butt and get a job because it's not going to come forever." Sounds lean—or mean—doesn't it?

First thing you see is security guards. It will become obvious as I tell the story why someone might flip out and get violent. The guard behind the desk directed me to the same "Reception" line as everyone else stood in. Darn, I thought there'd be someone who could do it right away because it was so simple. Luckily, there were only about six people ahead of me. As I waited, I observed.

Karen Wilhelm, "Welfare Waste," *Lean Reflections,* November 9, 2006, Reproduced by permission. http://leanreflect.blogspot.com/2006/11/welfare-waste.html.

Twenty People Enduring a Long Wait

To my left was a human inventory holding area—about 60 chairs, arranged in rows, with about 20 people occupying them. Occasionally, one of them would approach the desk to ask why the wait was so long. Between the clients and the workers there were about three people behind the desk who were supposed to deal with the flow, and they looked harried and sick of the whole thing.

Every few minutes, one of the people waiting would be called to the desk and some actually dispatched to see their social worker. Some of those waiting who pulled the andon cord [a cord used on manufacturing assembly lines to signal production to stop], so to speak, succeeded in getting their social worker paged or e-mailed a second time and were put back into the process flow.

Among the staff, there was a lot of walking around, a lot of paging and e-mailing of social workers, a lot of interruption when the social worker responded, a lot of waiting and a lot of frustration.

The Uncertain Drop Box

A couple of stories:

A woman in line behind me needed to get something to her social worker that day or her utilities were going to be cut off. There was supposed to be a drop box she could put it in, but naturally she didn't trust that process and wanted to put the envelope in the social worker's hand. I would too. But an unnecessary wait if the system worked. We all looked around, and eventually saw that there was a table with a slot in it with a dingy label saying "drop box," but there was no assurance that it was the right drop box or that anyone even emptied it on a regular basis.

When I got to the counter, the clerk was immediately interrupted by a message from a social worker, so she called the person who'd been waiting to the counter while I was shunted

Welfare

aside. This was a man in a wheelchair, apparently partially paralyzed, accompanied by a companion who had some sort of helper role. The clerk told him that the social worker said he didn't have an appointment, and that message seemed to mean that the man had waited for nothing and would have to come back. He held out a blank benefit application and tried to say that he just needed help filling it out.

The clerk admonished him for signing in on the appointment sheet. How would you know? I wouldn't. She asked, couldn't the other guy help him? The man said he couldn't. Then she said he'd have to wait while she found someone to help with the application. How many unnecessary obstacles can you count for both the clerk and the applicant?

Unclear Instructions

Back to me. I produced the form, which the volunteer liaison told me I could just have them sign upon seeing my driver's license. Of course, that turned out not to be true. I needed to show my social security card. She repeatedly asked if I had it, or had something else with my social security number on it. All I could do was repeatedly say with a helpless note in my voice that I didn't, and I hadn't been told to bring it. (And most of us have heard that we shouldn't take anything with the number on it with us if we want to avoid identity theft, but I didn't want to say that. I didn't want to make her mad; she was the only person who could help me avoid another wait.)

She was clearly frustrated and said she had told the school before that people needed both forms of identification. She thrust a piece of paper toward me that had a few lines of text, one of them covered with magic marker, and wrote at the top in big capital letters, "ALOUD 1 WEEK," with a phone number at the bottom and the name of the school. Apparently I was expected to take that back to the school so they'd stop making the mistake. How did it become my problem? What-

Other Perspectives on Welfare

ever. She grumbled and decided to accept my form anyway. Oh, I could come back and get it Monday. Maybe that's what "ALOUD 1 WEEK" meant.

Taxpayer Money Is Wasted

My empathy for all the people in this situation was growing. It was frustrating, to the point of anger, and humiliating for the people who needed help. There are a lot of people getting laid off here in Michigan, and more people like this man in the wheelchair who shouldn't be subjected to these obstacles and long waits. I'm sure there were a couple of malingerers or cheats among them, but that's beside the point.

And, it's taxpayer money being wasted. Someone probably thought that laying off some FIA [Family Indepence Agency] workers would be a good way to save money. Thus, inadequate resources to keep up with the process flow.

What percentage of people would at this point, leave the office and never come back, and never even tell the school why they dropped out?

All This and Still Unfinished

I still needed to get three references. And, since I needed a TB [tuberculosis] test, the liaison had taken me to the clinic after I met with her (good) to get part one of the test, and I needed to go back to have the test read.

More potential drop-outs from the volunteer recruiting process.

I decided to calmly keep on, and besides, I was getting interested in all the ways these processes could be improved—not that anyone was likely to care. . . .

Oh yes, it does say on the very wordy "How to complete the Volunteer Application" to take your social security card when you "drop off" the form at the FIA. The reason for the check is to ensure "that there are no pending or substantiated child abuse charges against you." I agree that protecting the

67

Welfare

girls is paramount. But why not add the instructions to the badly Xeroxed page that the FIA form appears on?

It's a lesson in going to the gemba [observing the process firsthand]. You can't really understand the process until you've walked it.

SOCIAL ISSUES FIRSTHAND

CHAPTER 3

Creating Welfare Policy

From Civil Rights to Welfare Rights

Marian Kramer, as told to Alan Govenar

Born in Baton Rouge, Louisiana, in 1944, Marian Kramer was active in the fight for civil rights even as a child. Her determination to help end discrimination and poverty, and her own experiences as a welfare recipient, eventually led her to a cochairmanship of the National Welfare Rights Union. Alan Govenar is the founder of Documentary Arts, a nonprofit organization dedicated to the promotion of diversity and fresh perspectives. His books include The Early Years of Rhythm and Blues *and* Extraordinary Ordinary People.

In the following selection, Kramer recalls her 1965–2007 experiences in the fight for welfare rights, including receiving welfare herself and being threatened with jail time for supporting workers who fought the condemnation of their houses.

In 1965, we were told at WCO [West Central Organization, Detroit] that there was going to be a poor people's conference in Syracuse, New York. WCO organized a bus that December to take a busload of community folks to this poor people's conference in Syracuse, New York. This was quite an experience for us. We went on that bus trip, and when I got there, I saw some of the people that were in the civil-rights movement with me. And they requested that my husband and I and a few other people sit down with [sociology professor] Frances Piven and Richard Cloud [Piven's husband], who were thinking about the concept, along with [civil rights

Marian Kramer, Alan Govenar, *Untold Glory: African Americans in Pursuit of Freedom, Opportunity and Achievement.* New York: Harlem Moon, 2007. Copyright © 2007 by Alan Govenar. All rights reserved. Used by permission of Harlem Moon, an imprint of The Doubleday Broadway Publishing Group, a division of Random House, Inc, and from Alan Govenar for UK rights.

leader] George Wiley (who had been in CORE [Congress of Racial Equality] with me), to talk about the need to build a welfare-rights organization. But I could not commit, nor could my husband at that time, to organize directly for welfare rights. I told [George] we would help to organize some people to come to the meeting in Washington that he was talking about. A march was taking place from Cleveland to Columbus, Ohio, and they wanted people to be mobilized here [Detroit] or in Washington. So I started helping to do some cases here against the welfare department. I had never taken on the welfare department before. We began to have a committee that was dealing with nothing but social-services programs. So much was going on at that time. And after a couple of years, my husband decided he was going back to school to get a master's degree in social work. And I took the job at WCO and became an organizer. That's when I learned how to organize block clubs and organize against urban renewal. And then I had to face up to myself [and my own personal problems] a year later, and my husband and I separated.

Arrested for Defending Workers' Rights

Some ministers and all the rest of us were trying to save this particular community. I began to learn about condemnation court—how the city could condemn properties through the court system. Each step of the way, I was learning. But in 1966, we were facing federal penitentiary because in this area, Research Park (that Wayne State University was trying to get and use as a research area), the workers who lived in these homes took a stand and said, "We're not giving up our houses." And we decided as an organization, because we had been working over there with them, that we would support them. And the police arrested us. I got arrested with a gang of ministers from different denominations. And they put a felony on us, felonious assault and battery. Eventually, through our organizing, the charges were dropped, but the judge really didn't want to drop them. He wanted to send us to the penitentiary for seven years.

During the rebellion [the Detroit race riot of 1967], I was out there trying to help save our community, making sure the young people didn't get hurt. Later, we built the League of Revolutionary Black Workers, which was in a lot of the major factories around here, as well as in about fourteen high schools. The Black Student United Front and some of the elementary schools and some of the hospitals and clinics and some of the social workers and churches were all a part of the League of Revolutionary Black Workers. Our main goal was to get some justice for blacks within the factories and within the schools.

A Hotbed of Activity

At the time of the rebellion, there was a lot of police brutality. A lot of injustice was going on at the time. Well, there was an after-hours joint down on 12th Street, which is now named Rosa Parks Avenue. And there was a lot of harassment by the police. And finally, the people just got fed up with them, and after they had brought everybody out on 12th Street that night, and people said they just got fed up and started rebelling.

Rosa Parks worked over in Conyers's office, Congressman John Conyers's office. I was in the South during the bus boycott. She had her own little organization. And when I came up here [around December 1964] to get married, people asked me if I would escort Rosa Parks around Detroit—[voting rights activist] Fannie Lou Hamer wanted us both to go around together. Fannie Lou Hamer was very instrumental in the civil-rights movement. Detroit was and still is a hotbed of activity.

Asked to Take a Job with Welfare Rights

Well, around 1970, I was approached by some folks about going to New York and helping Welfare Rights to reconstitute itself. Welfare Rights had grown to over 100,000 members. I had maintained my membership in Welfare Rights, although I was not doing direct organizing. I had helped in WCO and made sure WCO had Welfare Rights as a part of it and helped organize the Welfare Rights in Jeffries Public Housing [in Detroit]. George Wiley had called me and said, "Marian, why don't you come on staff of Welfare Rights?"

I said, "George, you know how we organize, to make sure that the people who are in control are the membership. I don't think the leadership in this area is going to appreciate that. And they're not going to hire me. So it's best that I stay where I am." And so I was not hired, but I still supported and worked directly with Welfare Rights.

In 1975, I started working full-time with Welfare Rights. Before then, I was active in our Welfare Rights group and maintaining another job. But when I had my baby in 1970 and I was separated from my husband, I got on aid, and I had to personally confront the welfare system. I had to go in there and fight it to try to get some help.

The Second Welfare Rights Convention

I went to the Welfare Rights second convention. It was held here in Detroit. And my cousin Charlie Granger, who had been a football player at one time, and his wife, Barbara, called me and said they were coming up to the convention, because Charlie was working with Welfare Rights also. And that's when I first met Annie Smart from Louisiana. They talked me into going to the convention—"Come on, Marian"—I wasn't going to go. I said, "Since it's at Wayne State, I'll go over there to this convention." So I went, and I got hooked again. I was so proud of these women, these women that were not only able to articulate their problem. These women were strong; these women were ready to fight for their children to have a better life—and not only for their children but for poor children throughout the country—to fight the battle against poverty.

To New York

So when I was asked in 1975 if I would go to New York and help bring recognition to Welfare Rights on a national level, I said, "Yes, I will come. And I will get on aid and try to organize if I don't get a job." And I went to New York, and I started organizing. I took the challenge, and I went there and began to do that work without any salary or anything. I got on welfare because Welfare Rights did not have any paid staff at the time. The second year, I was able to get a grant to go to school, which paid for a lot, coupled with my welfare check, because at that time, the grant was waived as far as trying to obtain an education. So I had a busy life in New York. We started Welfare Workers for Justice because of the economic crisis in the factories—a lot of people were laid off. We began to see a trend that technology was creeping in. And the reserve army of unemployed was beginning to join the permanent army of unemployed. And so what we did in New York was, we didn't go to using the name New York Welfare Rights Organization. We selected the name Welfare Workers for Justice because our attitude was that we were all workers. Some of us were temporarily unemployed, in low-paying jobs or no jobs at all.

Problems with the Welfare System

The first thing I did with Welfare Workers for Justice was to take on what I was a victim of myself. I made sure I went through the process. And that was standing out in the cold at four-thirty in the morning, trying to be one of the first people to get an application into the Department of Human Resources there in New York. People would be freezing to death. I mean, they would take the garbage cans and light them up where people could be warm. The fire department would come out, put the fires out, and people would light them back up because they needed heat out there. This was to be able to be in line to get some services from the welfare department.

People were experiencing a lot of unemployment at the time, so those lines were long. It took us several days to try to get some help from the welfare department or to begin to process our case. But if you were eligible, you had to go through a process of a face-to-face redetermination every six months, which was very degrading. It was like being on probation. It was like starting all over again. So that began my challenge—how to eliminate this face-to-face redetermination. Even the vets had to go through it. And we were successful in getting redetermination eliminated in New York. Then we took on the whole question around being SSI [Supplemental Security Income] recipients, which included a lot of senior citizens. They were eating dog food because they could not afford any food. There was a thing in New York which said the state could opt out, and it's still there—either give food stamps or give ten dollars in their check. They opted to give the ten dollars to cover food for folks each month in their check. So dog food was more cost-efficient to the seniors than the actual food itself.

Helping a Convict's Family

Another struggle that we took on when I was there involved a young kid who was hit by a car. He was an Italian American. And his mother didn't know what to do because of the fact that her husband was usually the person that took care of everything in their particular culture. And her husband was in Attica—you know, the prison. It hit the news, how the child might not live. Well, I got on the phone that night and found out where I could get more information concerning this family. And I was able to get them to let the father out for three days to check on the family, and I was able to talk to the father, and I told him to meet me at Welfare Rights at the Department of Human Resources the next day, and we'd try to help him get some help for his family. And we did.

Moves and Changes

When I first moved to New York, I lived in Park Slope. My whole time in New York, I lived in Brooklyn—Park Slope, Crown Heights. I was in New York for two and a half years. And then I went back to Detroit, and I've been here ever since. I figured if we're going to make this organization successful, we need to be around organized labor. And what better place than Detroit. And I moved back here, and at the same time, I began to date General Baker Jr., who is now my husband (and whom I had met some years earlier when I started organizing in Detroit).

Welfare Rights was built on the heels of the civil-rights movement, and Welfare Rights was being built at the time the Dodge Revolutionary Union Movement (DRUM) was built on the heels of the rebellion. It was the spark that started a lot of union movements within the various factories here in Detroit. We were in fourteen different high schools with the Black Student United Front. We spoke to the problems that black students were facing in these schools in Detroit, as well as those many were facing in the auto plants.

Welfare Rights and NOW

In the 1990s, Faith Evans, who had been in Welfare Rights and had been working with the National Organization for Women [NOW], and I sat down and talked about whether Welfare Rights and NOW could work together. Patricia Ireland was the president at the time. And I said, "Why should we? We have been treated so bad in the past by not only different women's organizations—be they black, white, green or yellow—why should we stick our necks out again?" I said, "Look, our meeting would not just consist of the women, but it would be some men who are in leadership also." So NOW helped, through Faith Evans, to raise funds and brought in twenty-five of us to meet with them. And that was a hell of a meeting that took place between us and NOW. And those women were in tears when they heard how we had been treated in the past. And we agreed to work together. We ended up being a part of all their marches after that, because they knew we had a stand also for choice [to get an abortion]. I told them, "Your overall struggle is for choice. The women we represent, they don't even have an opportunity to make a choice because they don't have the economic base. And yes, we're going to fight that the federal government should be responsible for women to be able to have that right to choice, whether or not they want to have a baby, or whether or not they want to have an abortion. That is our position. But you have to also fight with us." And we became instrumental in a lot of NOW's conventions.

Welfare Rights and Community Partnership

I'm codirector, executive director, of Detroit NFI, Detroit Neighborhood and Family Initiative, and I'm working to build a back-to-basics community partnership. And a component of that is welfare-rights organization. I'm the chairperson, co-president, of the National Welfare Rights Union.

If this country claims that it cares about the well-being of children, it's a lie. It's a lie, and we're here to say that that is a lie. So I'm going to stay in this fight. I just tell people, "Bury me with my boots on." One of our women, Guida West, wrote the book *The National Welfare Rights Movement*. And she not only wrote it, Guida was a part of it and still is. She lives in New York. Guida is almost in her eighties. We have another woman there in Texas that's been very instrumental in welfare rights and one of our heroes, Irena Edwards, who lives in Houston. Irena is in her eighties and in declining health, but Irena kept Houston on the map. Originally from Opelousas, Louisiana, but she's a Texan now. So these women still exist around the country. There are not too many of us that started out at the beginning of the movement. But I've been fortunate.

Welfare

Still Plenty of Battles to Fight

What keeps me going? I've been fortunate to have known and learned a lot from these women and from the men that have been a part of fighting against injustice and fighting for a better world that we know can happen. We have enough here in this country to make sure—we can build houses on the assembly line in less than forty-five minutes, but yet the homeless population is constantly growing. Education is not the priority it needs to be. Quality education for everybody? We don't have it. So Welfare Rights has always stood on the premise—not always, but we framed the program back in the eighties—that said we wanted universal health care. We have changed that now. We want health care to be nationalized. We're calling for the nationalization of water now because right now [2005] in Highland Park, Michigan, where I live, they're trying to privatize our water. Our city is being run by nonelected officials. We've been taken over by the state. And if you want to learn something, see how they're moving on Detroit and all the other cities in the state of Michigan; this is what they're trying to do everywhere. We pay the highest water bill in the nation, probably in the world, in this little city. Forty thousand people in the city of Detroit, in one year's time, had their water shut off. We know that we don't have to live this way. And that's what keeps me going. I don't want my children—I don't want anyone's children—to have to live like that.

The Struggle to Pass Welfare Reform

Ron Haskins

Now codirector of the Center on Children and Families at the Brookings Institution (an independent research and policy institute in Washington, D.C.), Ron Haskins served fourteen years on the Ways and Means Committee's Resources Subcommittee in the U.S. House of Representatives. He has also been a welfare policy advisor to President George W. Bush, and, before that, a principal architect of the Personal Responsibility and Work Opportunity (Welfare Reform) Act, which became law in 1996 after a lengthy Congressional battle.

In the following viewpoint, Haskins describes firsthand the July 1996 struggle to mold a drastic and long-contested welfare reform bill into a form acceptable to the majority of Congress. Shortly after the events recounted here, the bill passed as the Personal Responsibility and Work Opportunity (Welfare Reform) Act of 1996.

The Republican [state] governors had been restive ever since the Senate Finance Committee marked up their version of the [welfare reform] bill on June 26 [1996]. In the days following the Finance markup, I talked frequently about the Finance bill with LeAnne Redick and Gerry Miller of [Michigan governor John] Engler's staff as well as other state officials. My general aim was to assure them that we would use the House-Senate conference to change many of the provisions they didn't like in the Senate bill. My assurances seemed to placate them somewhat, but they kept calling and telling me that the governors were getting increasingly upset.

Ron Haskins, *Work over Welfare: The Inside Story of the 1996 Welfare Reform Law*, Washington, DC: Brookings Institution Press, 2006. Copyright 2006 © Brookings Institution. All rights reserved. Adapted with permission.

Welfare

So I worked with LeAnne and others to develop a list that we could use to guide [Florida Republican congressman E. Clay] Shaw's actions during the House-Senate conference and that LeAnne and Gerry could use with Engler and the other governors to show that we knew their concerns.

Addressing the Difficulties

Eventually my list included twenty-six items that, for Shaw's use, I divided into three categories by degree of difficulty (easy, medium, hard) in resolving. Most of the items concerned provisions that in some way limited the governors' flexibility. Governors still did not like the maintenance-of-effort requirements [for states to spend their own money on welfare] or either the welfare block grant or the child care block grant; they wanted us to drop even the modest requirements on child care regulations (most of which had been in the law since 1990); they wanted to reduce Medicaid coverage; they were furious about the stepped-up penalties the Senate bill required them to impose on welfare recipients who did not meet the work requirement and even more upset by the [Texas senator Phil] Gramm provision that imposed huge penalties on states that failed to meet the work requirement year after year; and they still demanded to count all families that left welfare against the work requirement. In our view these were serious issues but hardly the deal busters governors were labeling them.

Fearing that the governors were getting too upset over these and similar issues, we set up a conference call involving [Republican Speaker of the House Newt] Gingrich, [Senate majority leader Trent] Lott, Shaw, [Ways and Means Committee chairman Bill] Archer, [House Commerce Committee chair Tom] Bliley, [Senate Finance Committee chair] Bill Roth and several Republican governors, including Engler. The call took place at five o'clock on July 9, the day before Gingrich's leadership group was scheduled to take up the issue of separating the welfare and Medicaid bills, the discussion of which was another reason for the conference call. The governors were sour, saying they now didn't like either the Medicaid bill or the welfare bill. The welfare provision they seemed to dislike the most was the Gramm penalty provision on states. The call was not a total loss, however, because the governors agreed that separating the welfare reform and Medicaid bills was necessary if we were to move the welfare bill through Congress. Equally important, it was obvious for the first the time that Lott believed the bills should be separated. But I knew when the call ended that the governors were not satisfied and that Engler was going to be increasingly difficult to keep happy.

Furor over Changes

On Sunday, July 14, five days after our conference call with the governors, I got a call at home from LeAnne, who was in Puerto Rico. The governors were in San Juan having their annual summer meeting, and LeAnne wanted me to know how furious they were with the developments on welfare reform. Their anger, she said, was directed mainly against the Finance Committee bill and the Gramm provision. [Press secretary] Ari [Fleischer], Shaw, Archer, and I had been working by phone on drafting a response to the president's Saturday radio address on welfare. We had ample opportunity to talk and exchange ideas about how to deal with the governors. LeAnne said that one of the ideas the governors were considering was traveling by private jet to meet with Shaw, who was campaigning in his Ft. Lauderdale district. We changed Shaw's schedule for both Sunday and Monday so he could meet with the governors in Ft. Lauderdale, but that plan was canceled when the governors couldn't get a plane. LeAnne called me at work early Monday morning and told me that the governors were still upset and insisted on seeing Shaw. So LeAnne and I set the meeting for nine-thirty the next morning, Tuesday, July 16, the day before the bill was scheduled for the House floor. Because the annual governors' meeting was still taking place, the governors sent only Governor [Mike] Leavitt of Utah to represent them at the meeting with Shaw in his Washington office. Leavitt showed up right on time with LeAnne and one other staffer. Shaw's secretary greeted them and ushered them immediately into Shaw's office, where Shaw and I, plus Shaw's welfare staffer Heather Lank, were waiting. I had already been in Shaw's office for at least half an hour reviewing with him why the governors were so upset. I brought copies of the twenty-six-item list that LeAnne and I had been developing so that we could prepare answers for all the complaints Leavitt was likely to raise.

Off to the "Worst Possible Start"

The meeting got off to a disastrous start. After an exchange of pleasantries, which lasted about five seconds, Leavitt, in a direct and almost heated fashion, told Shaw that he was speaking for all the Republican governors, who were ready to go public in denouncing the bill. Shaw sat quietly looking at Leavitt as he delivered his disquisition. When he finished, Shaw responded in an intense but fully controlled voice. The first thing he said was that Leavitt had gotten the meeting off to the "worst possible start." So we were going to start over and begin with history. Shaw said that he had personally worked with the governors since 1993, that he had carried their water in every hearing and meeting, that we had shared drafts of legislation with them sooner than we did with our own members, and that he had taken every phone call from and accepted every request to meet with governors and to address their meetings in Washington. He had even completely changed his schedule for the last three days so he could accommodate the governors' request for yet another meeting. Given this background, it was too late for governors to desert the process now. No governor was going to go public and denounce the bill we had created together. On the contrary, the purpose of this meeting, as of so many previous meetings with the governors, was to find out exactly what the governors were concerned about and to figure out ways that Shaw could help address these concerns.

Discussing the Issues

Leavitt seemed to be taken aback by the intensity of Shaw's response. He immediately said that Shaw had misinterpreted him, and that he had come to Shaw's office from Puerto Rico specifically to work things out. Leavitt then did a very wise thing—he suggested we talk about the specific issues that concerned the governors. He had come with the list prepared by LeAnne. Because LeAnne and I had been talking so much, our lists were very similar. We worked our way through his list, and Shaw, calling on one of his greatest assets as a lawmaker, showed sympathy for all the concerns raised by Leavitt. On most, as I had repeatedly assured LeAnne, Shaw actually agreed with the governors and on many he felt we could achieve at least part of what the governors wanted during the House-Senate conference. By the time the meeting ended, Leavitt had clearly communicated the governors' concerns about the Finance Committee bills, some of whose provisions (like the maintenance-of-effort requirements) were also in the House bill and were certain to be part of the final legislation. But there seemed little doubt that Leavitt, like the other governors Shaw had dealt with, left with the belief that Shaw would get everything he could for them. Even more notable was the rise of good feelings during the meeting—and it is good feelings that create and maintain a coalition.

Work on the Bill Continues

Once again, Shaw had made the best of a difficult situation, but we didn't have much time to feel good. Besides, Shaw and I both knew that we had not heard the last from the governors. Neither of us had any doubt that Engler would be a constant presence in Washington until the final bill was passed, and to some extent we welcomed it because our views were so similar to those of the governors. While Governor Leavitt went off to meet with people, I dashed to Legislative Counsel to work some more on the bill. We were scheduled to be on the house floor the next day. After meeting with Jim Grossman in the Legislative Counsel's Office to review the bill and make a few more changes, I returned to our Rayburn office and, along with my staffers Matt Weidinger and Cassie Bevan, began writing speeches for the floor debate. LeAnne called about setting up a meeting with Shaw, [Congresswoman Nancy] Johnson, and others to discuss several issues that we had touched on in the meeting that morning. Because the bill could be on the floor the next day and we were trying to get as many issues settled as possible before clearing the bill for the floor, we decided to try to meet that very day.

Last-Minute Meeting

As it turned out, everyone could meet at three-thirty. This was perfect timing, because Shaw and I had to be at a meeting of the House and Senate leaders at four o'clock to begin discussing the issues we knew would have to be compromised between the House and Senate when we melded the two bills in the House-Senate conference. A tight schedule like this would force everyone to be on time and to have a focused discussion. At the appointed hour, Governors Leavitt and Engler met with Shaw, Johnson, and Mike Castle of Delaware, a former Republican governor, in Nancy Johnson's office. Two items dominated the discussion. On the first, we had earlier agreed to allow governors to transfer funds among the new Temporary Assistance for Needy Families (TANF) block grant that would replace AFDC [Aid to Families with Dependent Children] the newly expanded child care block grant, and the Title XX block grant that had been in the law since 1981. Democrats, and some Republicans, including Johnson and

Castle, had complained that there should be limits to the amount of transferring that states could do. Unlimited transfers would give too much power to the states and would allow them to completely avoid congressional intent in creating the three separate programs. We agreed to place a limit on transfers out of the block grants and to insert language stating that any funds transferred to Title XX were to be spent only on children (or families with children) with incomes under 200 percent of the poverty level.

Johnson Stands Firm on Medicaid

The second big issue was Medicaid coverage, which continued to plague us even after the Medicaid block grant had been dropped. Johnson was determined that no child would lose Medicaid coverage because of welfare reform. Once she took this position, I never doubted that it or something very close would be in the final bill, and our planning was based on the assumption that we would have to sell broad Medicaid coverage to the governors. Under the Medicaid block grant, governors would have been able to reduce coverage. Thus I expected that the governors, having lost the Medicaid block grant, would be determined to fight for looser language that would allow them the "flexibility" to reduce the number of families and the length of time that states would have to provide Medicaid to families leaving welfare. But to my surprise, Engler was willing to cover nearly all families for a year after they left welfare if we would insert a provision that states could deny Medicaid coverage to anyone who refused to work if the state found them a job. Shaw asked Johnson and Castle if they could accept this provision. Both said yes, and we had a deal—assuming that no one in the leadership or on the Commerce Committee had a major problem with it.

Preparing for the Next Hurdle

Shaw and I left promptly at four to hustle from Johnson's office in the Cannon Building to Archer's office in Room H-208 of the Capitol. Because Chairman Roth somehow did not get the word about the meeting, Shaw and Archer had a good discussion with [Oklahoma] Senator Don Nickles and Senator Gramm about the upcoming House-Senate conference. Without Roth we could not reach even tentative agreements, but it was nonetheless useful to talk with two of the senators we would be bargaining with in just a few days to produce a final bill. An important outcome of the meeting was that Shaw and I realized how strongly Gramm would push the issue of reducing the number of employees at HHS [U.S. Department of Health and Human Services] and how much reducing the number of bureaucrats resonated with other Republicans. So I called my friend Rich Tarplin at HHS, a former top staffer for [Connecticut] Senator Christopher Dodd, and asked him for a second time if the administration was worried about the Gramm provision. He said they were. They had been working on language that gave Gramm most of what he wanted but that had enough flexibility so that HHS could live with the provision. I told him to send us their language as soon as possible and I would see if Gramm's staff would accept it.

The Nature of a Bipartisan Bill

But now an even more difficult issue than the number of HHS bureaucrats was on the horizon. On major issues in Congress, the main show is usually a fight between the bills offered by the majority and minority parties. But over the years, I often worked with bipartisan groups that disrupted the main show by writing a compromise bipartisan bill that attracted enough votes to cause trouble for the majority. The goal of a bipartisan bill is generally not necessarily to actually win a vote on the floor, although occasionally these centrist groups might be able to pull off this dazzling feat. Rather, the goal is to attract enough votes so that the majority is forced to modify its bill to attract enough centrist votes to retain a majority. Psychology plays a role in this game. Just the threat of a centrist bill will often cause the majority to modify its bill by dropping extreme provisions or by adding moderate provisions favored by the centrists. Just before we conducted our subcommittee markup on June 12, we had learned that Mike Castle, an expert on welfare issues, was working with John Tanner, a moderate Democrat from Tennessee, to write a centrist bill. Like the [1995] bill by [Georgia Congressman] Nathan Deal before it, Castle-Tanner was modeled on our majority bill but with the edges removed. Shaw and I both regarded Castle-Tanner as a credible threat. But both of us were pleased that the bill was being written by Castle, who we knew would be straight-forward with us throughout the fight. In addition, we had worked often and well with Castle's senior staffers Paul Leonard and Booth Jameson. Both Shaw and I had also worked with Tanner when we were in the minority, especially on welfare and child care issues, and we had a great deal of trust in Tanner and his staff as well.

Making a Deal

Not surprisingly, we found out about the bill because Castle had Booth, his main welfare staffer, call me to tell me that Castle intended to work on a bipartisan bill with Tanner. Castle and Tanner hoped to bring their bill to the floor as a substitute for our bill, perhaps with the blessing of the Democratic leadership, unless we modified our bill along the lines they suggested. To discuss Castle's concerns, we met with him for nearly an hour on July 11. The next day Castle sent us a letter outlining the major changes in our bill that were discussed during the meeting, including strengthening the maintenance-of-effort requirement, providing states with an additional $3 billion in guaranteed funding to support their welfare-to-work programs, eliminating the optional Food Stamp block grant, and making several changes that would soften the noncitizen provisions, especially for children. After receiving the letter, Shaw and I were certain that the changes we could offer would not be enough to convince Castle to give up his effort to craft a bipartisan bill. Shaw concluded that the Castle-Tanner bill would become a formidable opponent of our bill but that it would be impossible and unwise to try to kill the bill outright. Our plan was to cut a deal with Castle: we would support his right to bring his bill to the floor as an amendment in the nature of a substitute for our bill if he would speak in favor of our bill and vote for it if we defeated his bill. We also intended to ask him to try to get his supporters to vote for our bill after his had been defeated. This strategy, which we discussed with Castle, was a little risky (what if his bill passed?), but Shaw and I were confident that we would prevail.

Talent's Concerns

Jim Talent [Republican representative from Missouri] was not as confident about this strategy as Shaw and I were. During the two years and more that Shaw and I had been working with Talent as we fought, at first against each other but now side-by-side, to write and enact a strong welfare reform bill, Talent and I had developed a solid working relationship. I kept him well informed of important developments, usually by talking with him at meetings of the Republican Conference or by phone. I also spoke frequently with his welfare staffer, Kiki Kless, and with Robert Rector of the Heritage Foundation, with whom Talent and his staff were working closely. As the floor debate neared and Castle looked for other members to support his bill, Talent became concerned that Castle might be making too much headway and might be trashing our bill, something Castle had promised not to do. At nine in the morning of July 17 the Republican Conference met in Room HC-5 in the basement of the Capitol to make final plans for the impending floor debate on welfare reform. The meeting was actually a kind of pep rally, with at least 150 members in attendance amid a somewhat raucous atmosphere. During the meeting Talent paced back and forth in a small storage room adjoining Room HC-5; it was possible to talk in the storage room without disrupting the proceedings in HC-5. By leaving the door open, it was also possible to simultaneously keep an eye on the proceedings. I kept going back to talk with Talent, but he was getting more and more upset worrying that Castle was trying to turn Republicans against our bill. At that very moment, Castle was engaged in what looked like intense discussions with two or three members. Shaw had worked very hard to maintain harmony among all the key players; the day on which we were scheduled to begin the final showdown on the floor was not a good time to allow dissension among our forces. So I told Talent I would go over and just ask Castle what he was doing. As soon as I approached Castle, I could tell that he was not even discussing welfare. Rather, he and the other members were discussing a totally unrelated bill. Hustling back to Talent with a big smile on my face, I told him Castle was not even discussing welfare. Talent then made a sincere and moving little speech to the effect that he was an overly suspicious and flawed individual. He concluded by saying, "God isn't finished with me yet." You can get a lot accomplished working with a guy like Talent.

Final Meeting Before the Floor Debate

God was not through with any of us yet. As we prepared for the floor debate, we had had a short and routine meeting with Republicans on the Rules Committee on July 16. We recommended that Castle-Tanner be allowed to come to the floor for debate and voting, but the decision on this issue was deferred. Only the Speaker could make a decision of this magnitude. To promote efficient use of available floor time, the Rules Committee decided to conduct two hours of general debate before publishing the final rule. Around four-thirty on July 17, David Hobson of Ohio, who was on both the Appropriations and Budget Committees, came to the floor and asked

Welfare

unanimous consent to once again start a general debate on welfare reform, with the Budget Committee controlling the time. There was no objection (an early sign that Democrats were mellowing on welfare reform), and [Budget Committee chairman John] Kasich was soon recognized to initiate debate. The debate was still partisan and somewhat negative, but it was a taffy pull compared with the previous floor debates.

Final Changes and Amendment

As the afternoon wore on, Shaw and I met with Gingrich, [Rules Committee] chairman [Gerald] Solomon, and several members and staffers from Gingrich's office and the Rules Committee in Solomon's office adjacent to the Rules Committee hearing room on the third floor of the Capitol. The leadership had decided that there would be a relatively simple rule: inserted into the bill would be a Republican amendment to convey our agreements with the governors; a batch of technical changes; and an amendment, sponsored by Kasich, that strengthened work requirements in the Food Stamp program. In addition, as always, Democrats would be given the right to offer a motion to recommit either with or without instructions. Gingrich invited us to the meeting because he wanted to be sure that, if the Castle-Tanner bill were allowed to come to the floor for debate, we would have the votes to keep it from passing. After making his concern clear, and emphasizing again that the leadership wanted a simple rule, he asked us whether we should allow the Castle-Tanner substitute to come to the floor. Shaw and I simultaneously answered yes. After some quizzing by Gingrich about whether we could hold our votes against Castle-Tanner, and assurances from us that we could, he agreed. Now the rule was set, and the meeting was quickly adjourned—although Gingrich still had enough doubt that he later sent a signed letter to every member of the Republican caucus reminding them that Castle-Tanner had to be defeated. The next morning, July 18, Porter Goss of Florida, representing the Rules Committee, appeared on the floor of the House and was recognized by the Speaker to place the rule before the House. After an hour of relatively mild debate, the rule was passed overwhelmingly on a vote of 358 to 54, another welcome sign that Democrats were mellowing.

The Most Constructive Debate for Welfare Reform

Following general debate, there was a decorous discussion of the Kasich amendment to require work of able-bodied adults on Food Stamps who had no children. The Kasich amendment was adopted on a vote of 239 to 184, after which the House turned to the Castle-Tanner substitute. Of the many hours of floor debate on welfare reform in 1995 and 1996, the Castle-Tanner debate was the most constructive. There was not a hint of name-calling, and several members gave impressive speeches based exclusively on their analysis of provisions in the bill. In accord with our agreement, both Castle and Tanner focused their remarks on the Shaw bill entirely on provisions they either did not like or considered to be lacking. The mild debate on Castle-Tanner indicated to those of us who had been through the debate in 1995 that much of the fire had gone out of the Democrats and that some of them were now, as Shaw had predicted in that first subcommittee markup back in February 1995, characterizing our bill in terms that would allow them to support it later. Liberal Democrats were realizing that a bill they despised had a good chance of becoming law and could well be signed by their president.

As soon as the allotted hour of debate had expired, the speaker announced a recorded vote. Within a minute or so, Shaw was joined on the floor by Gingrich, [Republican Conference head Dick] Armey, and [Texas congressman Tom] DeLay, all of whom began lobbying Republicans to stick with Shaw and not support Castle-Tanner. They didn't have to say much. Just seeing the leaders on the floor showed our mem-

Welfare

bers how high the stakes were and, after nearly eighteen months of party discipline, they knew unity was the key to legislative success. Once again, Republican discipline was superb: Castle-Tanner got only 168 votes in favor, 258 against. Only nine Republicans voted for the bill, and its fate was sealed when thirty-six Democrats also voted against it. As the vote proceeded, the smile on Shaw's face kept getting bigger and bigger. After one more vote, on which we defeated the motion to recommit by 220 to 203, the House moved to final passage without further debate. [President Bill Clinton signed the final version into law on August 22.]

Encouraging Welfare Recipients to Take Responsibility for Their Future

George W. Bush

President George W. Bush, in this speech to welfare-to-work graduates, praises the welfare reform law of 1996 for reducing the number of citizens on public assistance, helping people develop greater personal responsibility, and encouraging the poor to build better lives for themselves. He also argues for further reforms requiring longer work (or education) hours for welfare recipients; for greater funding of state-based programs and of job-related training and expenses; and for faith-based initiatives.

The welfare law of 1996 has enabled millions of Americans to build better lives—better lives for themselves and better lives for their families and, hence, better lives for our country. The time has come to strengthen that law, and that's what I want to talk about today....

The reforms of the 1990s recognized that people on welfare are not charges of the state: they're citizens of this country, with abilities and aspirations. Both parties in Congress realize that welfare system as we knew it sapped the soul and drained the spirit from our citizens. They came together, the people of both parties, to put an end to the culture of dependency that welfare had created.

The obligation of Government did not end with just mailing of a check, and that's important for our citizens to realize. Men and women deserved a chance to learn new skills. That was an obligation of Government, to help people learn, to use their talent so that they could realize dreams, to gain the ful-

George W. Bush, "Remarks to Welfare-to-Work Graduates: January 14, 2003," *Weekly Compilation of Presidential Documents*, v. 39, no. 3, January 20, 2003, pp. 66–68.

fillment of sense of purpose that comes with striving and working and providing for their own families.

Americans Are Better Off Since Welfare Reform

Since welfare was reformed millions of Americans have shared in this experience. Their lives and our country are better off. Today [in 2003], more than 2 million fewer families are on welfare—2 million fewer than in 1996. It's a reduction of 54 percent. That's a number, but behind each number is a life. And that's important to recognize. In Washington, we spend a lot of time talking about numbers. And that's okay. It's kind of a measuring tool. But we've also got to remember, with each number is somebody's aspiration and hope.

During the period from 1996 to 2001, the percentage of welfare recipients who are working tripled. That's incredibly positive news. According to the most recent census data, the poverty rate amongst Hispanic children has reached the lowest level in over 20 years. The poverty rate among African American children is the lowest ever recorded. There's a correlation, it seems like to me.

Behind these statistics are great personal achievements. Adversity has been overcome, and lives have changed forever. I met people all round our country who can share their stories of hard work and fighting odds that have been stacked against them. Moms and dads who battled addiction and have overcome addiction. Folks who have had trouble holding a job and found out that they could and realized their dreams.

Helping Change Lives for the Better

The welfare law is a success because it puts Government on the side of personal responsibility, and it has helped people change their life for the better, helped people realize their dreams, helped people help themselves. That's one of the key principles of the law that makes a lot of sense, that has helped make this law effective.

Last year [2002], the House of Representatives passed legislation [the Personal Responsibility Work, and Family Promotion Act (PRWFPA)] to build on the successes of the 1996 welfare reform law. They did so because they want more Americans to know the pride and success that come from hard work. The law that passed the House required 40 hours of work each week. There was a serious requirement for work. Of the 40 hours, 16 of those could be used for job training or education and, when needed, treatment for addiction. In other words, part of the 40 hours was helping people help themselves. And that's an important aspect of any law that encourages people to go from welfare to work.

Planning for Further Reform

The House bill set an ambitious goal for States to have 70 percent of the welfare recipients working within a five-year period of time. We encourage them to think that way because we believe in setting a high bar. We believe in the best. We don't accept mediocrity. Some say it's asking too much. But a lot of those voices were the same ones that said the 1996 law was flawed. In other words, they have low expectations for what is possible in this society.

Skepticism is refuted every single day, however, when we meet the hard-won successes from former welfare recipients. That's the best case that we can make, those of us who believe in expecting the best and working hard to achieve the best.

We've got new data refuting skepticism as well. A study from the University of Michigan shows that in the States with the strongest work incentives, single parents have seen larger increases in income than in States with weaker work requirements.

Work is the key to success in helping families lift themselves out of poverty. It's the key to success for improving the lives of our children. And the strong incentives in the House bill will encourage work. Unfortunately, the Senate never was

Welfare

able to act on the House bill, so it died. [Additional PRWFPAs were proposed in 2003 and 2005. Neither became law.]

Calling on Congress to Make Welfare Reform Work

Today I want to remind the new Congress we have an obligation to reauthorize the welfare bill, welfare reform, to make it work. And so I'm calling upon both Houses to get after it. Let's get a new bill up, a bill in which the House and Senate have got to work closely to achieve the objectives that we have just set out, the idea of getting people to work, make them less dependent upon Government, to help people in need, so they can realize their dreams.

I also want Congress to provide $17 billion a year to help the States run their welfare programs and 4.8 billion a year to help pay for childcare. Of course, there's a funding obligation that goes with the idea of setting high standards and strong goals. And since the caseloads have fallen by half, the States will now have twice the resources to spend on welfare and job training and childcare.

See, back in 1996, they were spending $7,000 per family to help people get to work. Under this budget request, the expenditure will be $16,000 per family. If $7,000 was good enough in 1996, it seems like $16,000 is good enough into '03 to help people get ahead.

Looking Far Ahead

It's important for Congress to authorize funding not just for next year but for the next 5 years, so that people who are working to help people understand there's a steady stream of funds that will help with the planning.

It's also important for Congress to work with us [the executive branch] to get a faith-based initiative going. I did a lot through an Executive order the other day that said faith programs will not be discriminated against at the Federal level. But the faith-based initiative is a part of welfare reform. It's one thing to help a person get the job skills necessary, but a lot of times we need to help people with their hearts and their souls. And the only place to find that help is in the faith-based community. And so, therefore, I'm still going to stay strong on the faith-based initiative, because I know of the hope and promise found in our churches and synagogues and mosques—hope and promise that can't be duplicated at the Federal level. . . .

Reemployment Accounts

And the other thing we can do is to do a better job for unemployed Americans through what I call Reemployment Accounts. These accounts will provide up to $3,000 per person to help pay for training, childcare, moving expenses, or other costs of finding a job. It provides incentive for people who are looking for work. If you find a job before the $3,000 runs out, then you get to keep the remainder, the balance. In other words, it's additional money to help people find work. It's money on top of the current system.

It's money that will recognize that power is best when it's disbursed to the people we're trying to help. It will help States on the frontlines of where there's unemployment or chronic unemployment. It's a good idea. I hope Congress acts as quickly as possible. I mean, the idea is that we want to help people. That's what we ought to do in America. We want to help people who, in this land of plenty, have overcome some incredibly tough times because of the lack of things, sometimes the lack of love, sometimes the lack of help, sometimes the lack of education. In a land where we've got an awful lot, there are still a lot of people who hurt, too many who hurt. And the role of Government is to help those good folks realize their potential. Everybody has got potential. Everybody has got worth. Everybody has got value. And the role of this Government is to help those people realize their value and worth.

The Food Stamp Program Benefits Low-Income Children

Nancy Montanez Johner

Nancy Montanez Johner, former director of the Nebraska Department of Health and Human Services, became undersecretary of food, nutrition, and consumer services (FNCS) for the U.S. Department of Agriculture (USDA) in August 2006. Since the 1990s, she has directed and administered programs designed to assist low-income citizens. She has a BS in social work from the University of Nebraska at Kearney.

In the following statement before the Subcommittee on Department Operations, Oversight, Dairy, Nutrition and Forestry, Johner testifies to the value of food stamps in ensuring healthy nutrition for low-income children and explains how FNCS is working to educate families on their eligibility for the program. She also outlines related programs (child nutrition, child and adult care, farm bills, supplemental nutrition for infants and their mothers) and issues (obesity, nutrition education), as well as FNCS's plans to increase benefits and savings opportunities for deserving recipients.

The FSP [Food Stamp Program] is the Nation's primary nutrition assistance program, increasing food purchasing power for households with little income and few resources by providing benefits that are redeemed at retail grocery stores across the country. Over 26 million low-income people make use of the program to help put food on the table.

This program provides substantial benefits to low-income families with children, helping them to stretch their buying

---

Nancy Montanez Johner, "Statement of Nancy Montanez Johner, Under Secretary, Before the Subcommittee on Department Operations, Oversight, Dairy, Nutrition and Forestry, House Committee on Agriculture," March 13, 2007. www.fns.usda.gov/cga/Speeches/CT031307.html.

power. About half of all food stamp recipients are children, nearly 80 percent of food stamp benefits go to households with children, and over 80 percent of all children who are eligible for benefits receive them. On average, households with children receive about $300 in food stamp benefits each month, with the amount varying based on the size and income level of the household. Food stamp households also benefit from nutrition education that is part of the program in every State—helping to promote thrifty shopping and healthy eating among food stamp clients.

The Food Stamp Program Works

The evidence is clear that the FSP makes an important difference in the lives of low-income children and families, and the others that it serves. With its nationwide standards for eligibility and benefits, it represents a national nutrition safety net for low-income families and individuals wherever they live. It is designed to expand automatically to respond to increased need when the economy is in recession and contracts when the economy is growing, making sure that food gets to people who need it, when they need it.

Perhaps most importantly, the FSP makes more food available to households that participate. Food stamp families are able to spend more on food than they would be able to without the program, and providing benefits that can be spent only on food increases total food expenditures more than providing an equal amount of cash would. In addition, there is evidence that program participation can increase the availability of nutritious food in the home.

To sum up, the Food Stamp Program works, and it works for children. That's why we're committed to ensuring effective program operations for all eligible people who wish to participate.

Raising Awareness About Food Stamps

To meet that commitment, we have implemented outreach activities such as the national media campaign. The number one reason that people do not apply for food stamp benefits is because they do not realize that they are eligible. The national media campaign seeks to raise awareness of the nutrition benefits of food stamps and encourage low income people to seek out more information about their eligibility for this important benefit. National media campaign activities primarily consist of radio advertising in areas of low participation.

The Food and Nutrition Service (FNS) also provides outreach materials for the Food Stamp Program including posters and flyers, as well as radio and television public service announcements, that State and local food stamp agencies and community and faith-based outreach providers can use in their local outreach efforts.

FNS has also awarded grants to community and faith-based organizations to implement and study promising outreach strategies. All of these outreach strategies are geared towards the working poor, including families with children, seniors, and legal immigrants, including citizen children of undocumented parents....

Other Major Nutrition Assistance Programs

I would be remiss if I did not mention the other major programs that I oversee which directly bear on this subject. The 15 domestic nutrition assistance programs administered by FNS work together to improve food security, fight hunger, and support healthy eating for low-income people across the Nation. The President's budget for Fiscal Year 2008 demonstrates the Administration's unwavering commitment to this mission by requesting a record level of $59 billion dollars for these vital programs, which serve one in five Americans over the course of a year. While these programs are designed to meet the needs of people of all ages who need assistance, they focus most strongly on the needs of children. In addition to food stamps, the major nutrition assistance programs include:

- The Child Nutrition Programs (CNP), including the school meals (lunch and breakfast) program, and the Child and Adult Care Food Program (CACFP), which support nutritious meals and snacks served to over 30 million children in schools, child care institutions, and after-school care programs. In addition, the Summer Food Service Program (SFSP) and parts of the National School Lunch Program provide nutritious food to children in summer camps and other settings in the summer months, when school is not in session.

- And for the youngest children and infants, we operate the Special Supplemental Nutrition Program for Women, Infants, and Children, or WIC. WIC addresses the special needs of at-risk, low-income pregnant, breastfeeding, and postpartum women, infants, and children up to five years of age. It provides 8 million participants monthly with supplemental food packages targeted to their dietary needs, nutrition education, and referrals to a range of health and social services; benefits that promote a healthy pregnancy for mothers and a healthy start for their children.

Promoting Healthy Lifestyles

Overweight and obesity are critical issues for every part of our population, and addressing those problems is most important early in life, when eating and other health-related behaviors are developed. The policies that shape the programs are aligned with the Dietary Guidelines for Americans, which are revised every five years to ensure that policy is based on current scientific and medical knowledge. And each major program promotes healthy eating and active lifestyles through nutrition education and promotion.

Nutrition education and services are provided to WIC participants in conjunction with other parts of the WIC benefit to improve birth outcomes and promote childhood immunization, and breastfeeding. Team Nutrition, a comprehensive, integrated plan to promote good nutrition through the Child Nutrition Programs, includes nutrition education materials for use in schools and technical assistance for food service providers. We also promote nutrition education across programs through the Eat Smart. Play Hard.™ Campaign, and by working with State agencies that operate the programs on State Nutrition Action Plans, to foster integrated cross-program strategies.

Educating Low-Income Families

Nutrition education efforts are not limited to the Child Nutrition Programs but are also provided by States to food stamp recipients. The program represents a prime opportunity to reach low-income children and families and encourage healthy practices that can last a lifetime.

The FSP clearly has been a major benefit to low-income households with children over the years. Children in the FSP have also benefited from the increased commitment to nutrition education as a component part of the Program. Considered an optional benefit on the part of States, spending in the area of nutrition education has increased over the last fifteen years. For example, in FY [fiscal year] 1992, FNS approved $661,000 for Food Stamp Nutrition Education (FSNE) efforts conducted by seven State agencies. [In 2007, FNS approved $275 million in federal funds for fifty-two State agencies to provide FSNE. It is important to note that FSNE plays a valuable role in helping to communicate the Dietary Guidelines for Americans to low-income audiences. This includes promotion of MyPyramid and its various iterations such as MyPyramid for Children and MiPiramide.

Materials for Food Stamp Mothers

To that end, FNS has also developed a series of nutrition education and promotional materials targeting women with children entitled Loving Your Family, Feeding Their Future: Nutrition Education through the Food Stamp Program. These materials are designed for Food Stamp mothers who may possess low-literate skills and who may be Spanish speakers. These materials can be used in any setting with similar target audiences, such as the WIC Program. The anticipated release date of these materials is May 2007.

The Food Stamp Nutrition Connection is a website designed to provide training and information resources to FSP nutrition educators, and it provides more than 150 nutrition education resources for children....

I would like to take a moment to outline several of our Farm Bill Proposals, especially those that would benefit households with children.

The 2007 Farm Bill Builds on Success

We are using the 2007 Farm Bill process to further improve program access and facilitate future self-sufficiency. The Administration's reform-minded and fiscally responsible proposals build on the success of the 2002 Farm Bill—raising food stamp participation rates among eligible populations, restoring eligibility for many legal immigrants, and providing new flexibility for States to tailor services to better serve their clients—with improvements in access, strong integrity, and careful stewardship of the taxpayer dollars. Let me outline some of the proposals that have particularly important impacts on families with children:

First, we want to strengthen efforts to integrate nutrition education into the Food Stamp Program by recognizing in the Food Stamp Act of 1977 that nutrition education is a component of the program and investing $100 million to establish a five-year competitive grants demonstration program targeted at developing and testing solutions to the rising rates of obesity. These grants will allow us to evaluate creative and innovative solutions in this complex area, such as point-of-sale incentives to purchase fruits and vegetables, increased access among food stamp recipients to farmers markets, and integrated initiatives that use multiple communication channels to reinforce key messages. These initiatives would include rigorous evaluations to identify effective strategies. This is important, as the Committee knows, because of the serious health threats of obesity and overweight threaten American citizens, but is even more critical when we consider the impact it has on our nation's children.

Increasing Program Access

Second, our proposals to increase program access that would affect families with children include:

- Eliminating the cap on the dependent care deduction—Current policy supports work or participation in work services by providing for limited deductions from the family's gross income associated with the cost of dependent care when determining food stamp eligibility and benefit amount: a cap of $200 per month for children under 2 and $175 for other dependent children is the current policy. The cap was set back in 1993. It is time to eliminate the cap, which would simplify State administration and help working families with children.

- Excluding the value of college savings plans from the resource limit—This proposal would expand the plans eligible for exclusion from the resource limit when determining food stamp eligibility and would simplify administration for the States. Most significantly, it supports working poor, encourages focused savings for children's futures, and recognizes that households should not have to deplete college savings plans in order to get nutrition assistance. This proposal will exclude from the resource calculation the value of certain college savings plans that the IRS recognizes for tax purposes, including 529 plans operated by most States.

- Excluding combat-related military pay—Enhanced pay from military deployment can sometimes cause families receiving food stamps to no longer be eligible for this assistance. This policy change would ensure that military families are not penalized for doing their patriotic duty. It supports the families of servicemen and servicewomen fighting overseas by ensuring that their families back home do not lose food stamps as a result of the additional deployment income. This proposal has been a part of the President's budget for several years and was first enacted in the 2005 Appropriations Act; this farm bill proposal would make this annual policy fix permanent.

- Encouraging savings for retirement—This proposal simplifies food stamp resource policy and makes it more equitable because under current law some retirement accounts are excluded and some are included. This proposal supports the President's Ownership Society Initiative, by increasing the ability of low-income people to save for retirement. It is expected, when fully implemented, to add approximately 100,000 persons to the program and to increase benefits by $592 million over 5 years. The majority of the new participants will be workers and their families, most with children, but also improves access for elderly.

The Budget for Fruits and Vegetables Should Be Increased

Third, beyond the $100 million in obesity-prevention grants, we also propose to improve nutrition for children by:

Welfare

- Adding new mandatory funding for the purchase of additional fruits and vegetables for use in the National School Lunch and Breakfast Programs. This $500 million of funding over 10 years represents a net increase in the total purchase of fruits and vegetables for school meals over levels available under any other authorities.

- Increasing Section 32 spending on fruits and vegetables by $2.75 billion over 10 years. This proposal will increase the availability of fruits and vegetables to low-income individuals and school children participating in nutrition assistance programs, and the consumption of these healthful foods can contribute to the improved health of program participants.

Food Stamps and the other USDA programs help us lead the fight against hunger, and the level of commitment to this task remains high. But we still know that there is more to do. We are continuing to improve program operations, get benefits to those who are already eligible, but do not participate, and keep our eye on program integrity in the process.

Organizations to Contact

The editors have compiled the following list of organizations concerned with the issues debated in this book. The descriptions are derived from materials provided by the organizations. All have publications or information available for interested readers. The list was compiled on the date of publication of the present volume; the information provided here may change. Be aware that many organizations take several weeks or longer to respond to inquiries, so allow as much time as possible.

Administration for Children and Families (ACF)
370 L'Enfant Promenade SW, Washington, DC 20201
Web site: www.acf.dhhs.gov

The ACF provides funding for assistance programs "that promote the economic and social well-being of families, children, individuals, and communities." It focuses on economic empowerment; community building; partnerships with front-line service providers, state agencies, and various associations; and issues involving immigrants and the disabled. The Web site provides details on many specific programs, such as Head Start and Temporary Assistance for Needy Families.

Business Interface, Inc.
19 South St., Baltimore, MD 21202
(410) 685-3935 • fax: (410) 685-3936
e-mail: info@businessinterfaceinc.com
Web site: www.businessinterfaceinc.com

Business Interface, Inc. (formerly the Welfare to Work partnership) was founded to help "move people from a life of dependency to self-sufficiency" by matching qualified job candidates, especially former welfare recipients, with struggling businesses. The Web site spotlights relevant businesses and organizations and includes a Current Projects page.

Welfare

Center on Budget and Policy Priorities
820 First St. NE, Suite 510, Washington, DC   20002
(202) 408-1080 • fax: (202) 408-1056
e-mail: center@cbpp.org
Web site: www.cbpp.org

The center works at the federal and state levels to inform public debates over proposed budget and tax policies and to help ensure that the needs of low-income families and individuals are considered in these debates. The center also develops policy options intended to alleviate poverty among working families and studies the impact of policies and programs affecting low- and moderate-income people. Research reports are available on its Web site.

Center for Nutrition Policy and Promotion (CNPP)
3101 Park Center Dr., 10th Fl., Alexandria, VA   22302-1594
(703) 305-7600 • fax: (703) 305-3300
e-mail: john.webster@cnpp.usda.gov
Web site: www.cnpp.usda.gov

CNPP, the research branch of the U.S. Department of Agriculture, publishes the Dietary Guidelines for Americans, as well as the Thrifty Food Plan, which helps determine food stamp benefits. Its Web site provides detailed research reports on nutritional needs, Americans' eating habits, and the costs of raising children.

Child Welfare League of America (CWLA)
2345 Crystal Dr., Suite 250, Arlington, VA   22202
(703) 412-2400 • fax: (703) 412-2401
Web site: www.cwla.org

The Child Welfare League of America is dedicated to developing and promoting programs in the interest of American children and families, especially the abused and neglected. CWLA, which comprises nearly eight hundred public and nonprofit agencies, publishes *Children's Voice* magazine and the *Child Welfare Journal*. Numerous research materials and publications can be accessed through its Web site.

Constitutional Rights Foundation (CRF)
601 S. Kingsley Dr., Los Angeles, CA   90005
(213) 487-5590 • fax: (213) 386-0459
e-mail: crf@crf-usa.org
Web site: www.crf-usa.org

This community-based nonprofit organization seeks to instill in America's youth a deeper understanding of citizenship through values expressed in the Constitution and Bill of Rights and to educate young people to become active and responsible participants in society. CRF members include teachers, community organizers, writers, and other concerned parties, who organize law and government and civic participation programs and provide printed materials to help youngsters understand the privileges and responsibilities of active citizenship. Its Web site includes a page on the history of welfare.

Economic Policy Institute
1333 H St. NW, Suite 300, East Tower
Washington, DC   20005-4707
(202) 775-8810 • fax: (202) 775-0819
e-mail: researchdept@epi.org
Web site: www.epi.org

The mission of this nonprofit think tank is to broaden the public debate about strategies to achieve a prosperous and fair economy. It publishes the *EPI Journal* and *EPI News*; archives and information on additional publications, including numerous reference materials on welfare, are posted on its Web site.

The Heritage Foundation
214 Massachusetts Ave. NE, Washington, DC   20002-4999
(202) 546-4400 • fax: (202) 546-8328
e-mail: info@heritage.org
Web site: www.heritage.org

The Heritage Foundation is a think tank whose mission is to formulate and promote conservative public policies based on the principles of free enterprise, limited government, individual freedom, and traditional American values. Its Web site includes numerous editorials and research links and a listing of policy experts.

MDRC
16 E. Thirty-fourth St., 19th Fl., New York, NY   10016-4326
(212) 532-3200 • fax: (212) 684-0832
e-mail: information@mdrc.org
Web site: www.mdrc.org

The Manpower Demonstration Research Corporation (simply MDRC since 2003) was created in 1974 by the Ford Foundation, in cooperation with various government agencies. Best known for mounting large-scale evaluations of real-world policies and programs targeted to low-income people and long known for its research on state welfare-to-work programs, MDRC focuses on five main policy areas: promoting family well-being and child development, improving public education, promoting successful transitions to adulthood, supporting low-wage workers and communities, and overcoming barriers to employment. Its Web site includes a "Welfare and Barriers to Employment" page.

National Center for Law and Economic Justice (NCLEJ)
275 Seventh Ave., Suite 1506, New York, NY   10001-6708
(212) 633-6967
e-mail: info@nclej.org
Web site: www.nclej.org

The National Center for Law and Economic Justice works to advance the cause of economic justice for low-income families, individuals, and communities across the country. The NCLEJ's publications include biennial reports on its progress in its mission and an organizational brochure, available on its Web site.

U.S. Department of Health and Human Services (DHHS)
200 Independence Ave. SW, Washington, DC   20201

(202) 619-0257; toll-free: (877) 696-6775
Web site: http://dhhs.gov

DHHS is the principal government agency for welfare, health education, and other human services. Its Administration for Children and Families sponsors Head Start and Early Head Start, child development programs that work to ensure adequate nutrition and school preparation for low-income children under five. The DHHS and ACF Web sites provide extensive health and safety information, along with materials on family issues and on financial assistance options for needy families.

U.S. Department of Housing and Urban Development (HUD)
451 Seventh St. SW, Washington, DC 20410
(202) 708-1112
Web site: www.hud.gov

HUD is a federal government agency that works to increase home ownership, support community development, and increase access to affordable housing free from discrimination. It partners with various faith-based and community organizations to leverage resources and improve its effectiveness on the community level. Extensive research material, including housing statistics and legal information, can be found on its Web site.

For Further Research

Books

Kenneth Brown with Patrick Borders, *From Welfare to Faring Well*. Southfield, MI: Ken Brown Ministries, 2005.

Rodney J. Carroll with Gary Karton, *No Free Lunch: One Man's Journey from Welfare to the American Dream*. New York: One World, 2002.

Pamela L. Cave, *The Other Side of Welfare: Real Stories from a Single Mother*. Sterling, VA: Capital, 2002.

Mona Charen, *Do-Gooders: How Liberals Hurt Those They Claim to Help—and the Rest of Us*. New York: Sentinel, 2004.

Jason DeParle, *American Dream: Three Women, Ten Kids, and a Nation's Drive to End Welfare*. New York: Viking, 2004.

Kathy Edin, *Making Ends Meet: How Single Mothers Survive Welfare and Low-Wage Work*. New York: Russell Sage Foundation, 1997.

Barbara Ehrenreich, *Nickel and Dimed: On (Not) Getting By in America*. New York: Metropolitan, 2001.

Ange-Marie Hancock, *The Politics of Disgust: The Public Identity of the Welfare Queen*. New York: New York University Press, 2004.

Joel F. Handler and Yeheskel Hasenfeld, *Blame Welfare, Ignore Poverty and Inequality*. New York: Cambridge University Press, 2007.

Richelene Mitchell, *Dear Self: A Year in the Life of a Welfare Mother*. Hayward, CA: NID, 2007.

Premilla Nadasen, *Welfare Warriors: The Welfare Rights Movement in the United States*. New York: Routledge, 2005.

Annelise Orleck, *Storming Caesar's Palace: How Black Mothers Fought Their Own War on Poverty*. Boston: Beacon, 2005.

Mark Robert Rank, *One Nation, Underprivileged: Why American Poverty Affects Us All*. New York: Oxford University Press, 2004.

David K. Shipler, *The Working Poor: Invisible in America*. New York: Knopf, 2004.

Martha Shirk and Anna Wadia, *Kitchen Table Entrepreneurs: How Eleven Women Escaped Poverty and Became Their Own Bosses*. New York: Basic Books, 2004.

John Stossel, *Give Me a Break: How I Exposed Hucksters, Cheats, and Scare Artists and Became the Scourge of the Liberal Media*. New York: HarperCollins, 2004.

Alan Weil and Kenneth Finegold, *Welfare Reform: The Next Act*. Washington, DC: Urban Institute, 2002.

Phyllis Williams, *From Welfare to Faring Well: Hang in There*. Enumclaw, WA: Pleasant Word, 2007.

Periodicals

America, "Food Stamps," July 30, 2007.

Cindy Ballard with Tracy Thompson, "I Was a Welfare Mom," *Good Housekeeping*, April 1999.

Heather Boushey, "The Needs of the Working Poor: Helping Working Families Make Ends Meet," testimony before the U.S. Senate, Committee on Health, Education, Labor, and Pensions, www.epi.org/content.cfm/webfeatures_viewpoints_boushey_testimony_20020214, February 14, 2002. Accessed January 9, 2008.

Welfare

Dennis Boyle, "In California, Welfare Ain't Broke: The Schwarzenegger Administration's Latest Tinkering Is Too Risky," *Los Angeles Times*, April 4, 2007.

Rosemary Bray, "So How Did I Get Here?" *New York Times Magazine*, November 8, 1992.

Steve Chawkins, "Choosing Their Lots in Life," Column One, *Los Angeles Times*, December 31, 2007.

Constitutional Rights Foundation, "Bill of Rights in Action: Welfare," www.crf-usa.org/bria/brial4_3.html#welfare, Summer 1998. Accessed January 8, 2008.

Gary Delgado and Menachem Krajcer, "Welfare's True Colors," *Nation*, October 28, 2002.

Gwen Filosa, "Millions in Food Stamps Go Unclaimed: 20,000 Eligible People Missed Aid, Study Says," *New Orleans Times-Picayune*, May 18, 2005.

Mike Franc, "States' Addiction to Welfare Corrupts Federalist System," *Human Events*, March 5, 2007.

Susan T. Gooden and Kasey J. Martin, "Welfare Reform: Government Does Matter (and Resources Do, Too!)," *Public Administration Review*, March/April 2005.

David Greenberg, Karl Ashworth, and Andreas Cebulla, "When Welfare to Work Programs Seem to Work Well: Explaining Why Riverside and Portland Shine So Brightly," *Industrial and Labor Relations Review*, October 2005.

Donna Hardina, "Guidelines for Ethical Practice in Community Organization," *Social Work*, October 2004.

Ron Haskins, "The Rise of the Bottom Fifth: How to Build on the Gains of Welfare Reform," *Washington Post*, May 29, 2007.

Sharon Hays, "Off the Rolls: The Ground-Level Results of Welfare Reform," *Dissent*, Fall 2003.

For Further Research

Anil Hira, "Time for a Global Welfare System?" *Futurist*, May/June 2007.

Caroline Howard, "Mom Paths—Moms Who Matter," *Working Mother*, www.workingmother.com/web?service=direct/1/ViewArticlePage/dlinkFullArticle &sp=S328&sp=100, May 2007. Accessed October 23, 2007.

Chris L. Jenkins, "Day-Care Advocates Push for Vouchers," *Washington Post*, December 20, 2007.

Alan Maass, "Working Poor in Bush's America: A Constant Struggle to Make Ends Meet," *Socialist Worker Online*, June 4, 2004, www.socialistworker.org/2004-1/502/502_02_WorkingPoor.shtml. Accessed October 12, 2007.

Kathy Martinez, "Interview with Betty Gray, Owner of Alice's Relaxing Bath Shop, Oakland, California," *Disability World*, May/June 2001, www.disabilityworld.org/11-12_01/women/grayinterview.shtml. Accessed October 12, 2007.

Lawrence Mead, "And Now, 'Welfare Reform' for Men," *Washington Post*, March 20, 2007.

Evelyn Nieves, "Job Market in West Virginia Defies Efforts to Reform Welfare," *Washington Post*, July 24, 2005.

Stephen Ohlemacher, "Public Aid Rolls Grow After Welfare Reform: Medicaid, Food Stamps Among the Programs for Poor Being Used More," *Houston Chronicle*, February 26, 2007.

Steven Pearlstein, "A Powerhouse for the Poor," *Washington Post*, May 4, 2007.

Katie Reckdahl, "Fewer Kids at Camp as Money Runs Dry: But 57 Programs Offer Summer Fun," *New Orleans Times-Picayune*, July 8, 2007.

Catherine Saillant, "Stamping Out Welfare Shame," *Los Angeles Times*, July 20, 2003.

Welfare

George Skelton, "A Welcome Debate on a Thorny Issue," *Los Angeles Times*, January 16, 1995.

Jackie Spinner, "Muslim Women Who Become Homeless Have Limited Options," *Washington Post*, December 29, 2007.

Scott Winship and Christopher Jencks, "Understanding Welfare Reform," Forum, *Harvard Magazine*, http://harvardmagazine.com/2004/11/understanding-welfare-re.html, November/December 2004. Accessed January 3, 2008.

Zoominfo.com "Former Welfare Mom to Carry Olympic Torch," www.zoominfo.com/people/Mitchell_Ramona_198106922.aspx, February 17, 2005. Accessed October 16, 2007.

Index

A

Adams, Gina, 57–63
Addiction
    descent into, 10
    struggles overcoming, 9, 94–95
    welfare families and, 94, 95
Aid To Families with Dependent Children (AFDC), 36, 39, 40, 84
Alcoholism, 16, 18, 32
American Public Human Services Association, 44
Appropriations Act (2005), 105
Appropriations Committee, 89
Archer, Bill, 80, 81, 85, 86
Armey, Dick, 91

B

Baker, General, Jr., 75
Benefits. *See* Welfare benefits
Bevan, Cassie, 84
Bipartisan legislation, 86–88
Black Student United Front, 72, 76
Bliley, Tom, 80
block grants
    child care/welfare, 80
    food stamps, 87
    Medicaid, 85
    Temporary Assistance for Needy Families (TANF), 84
    Title XX, 84–85
Brookings Institution, 79
Budget Committee, 89–90
Bureaucracy
    child-care subsidies, 62
    frustrations, 39–40, 43, 65–68
    opposition to, 74–75
    welfare system, 32, 33, 48, 53
Bush, George W., 93–97

C

Caseworkers. *See* Staff, welfare
Cash assistance system, 58
Castle, Mike, 84, 85, 87–89, 91
Castle-Tanner bill, 87–92
Challenges, future, for welfare system, 44–45, 95–97
Child and Adult Care Food Program (CACFP), 101
Childcare
    block grants, 80, 84, 85
    ethnic differences, 62–63
    need for, 47, 51
    quality issues, 59, 61–62
    residential facilities for girls, 64
    subsidies for, 51, 57–61, 96
    substandard conditions, 55
Child Care and Development Fund, 61
Childers, Mary, 16–21
Child Nutrition Programs (CNP), 101–102
Children, on welfare
    coping, 17–21
    Food Stamp Program benefits, 98–100
    impact of single parenting on, 38–39
    nutrition-assistance programs, 100–106
    poverty levels, 94
    protections for, 23, 34, 73, 77
Civil-rights movement, 70, 72, 76

117

Clinton, Bill, 92
Cloud, Richard, 70
College education
    racial differences, 29–30
    single-parent children, 38
College savings plans, and Farm Bill proposal, 104
Community Action Agency, 28
Condemnation court, 71
Congress of Racial Equality (CORE), 71
Conyers, John, 72
Crime
    welfare neighborhoods, 18–21
    welfare reform and, 35, 55

D

Dangers, in welfare neighborhoods, 18–21
Deal, Nathan, 87
DeLay, Tom, 91
Department of Human Resources, 74, 75
Dependency, on welfare, escape from, 16–21, 56, 93
Dependent care deduction, Farm Bill proposal and, 104
Detroit Neighborhood and Family Initiative (NFI), 77
Dietary Guidelines for Americans, 102
Documentary Arts (nonprofit organization), 70
Dodd, Christopher, 86
Dodge Revolutionary Union Movement (DRUM), 76
Drugs/drug addiction, 9, 32, 35, 47

E

Eat Smart. Play Hard. Campaign, 102
Education
    correlation with salary, 12
    nutrition, 100–104
    single-parent children, 38
    struggle/need, 26–27, 74, 78
    training programs and, 56, 93, 95
    welfare recipients, 12, 50, 97
Edwards, Irena, 77
Ehlers, Tracy Bachrach, 31–35
Ehrenreich, Barbara, 12, 13
Employment
    difficulties, 23–24, 74–75
    goals, 95
    incentives, 97
    requirements, 40, 50, 51, 59, 95
    shortages, 12–13, 32, 67
    training, 51, 57
    See also Minimum-wage jobs
Employment and training programs, 50–51, 57, 58
Engler, John, 79–81, 83–85
Ethnic issues
    child care patterns, 62–63
    welfare neighborhoods, 18–19, 20
Evans, Faith, 76

F

Faith-based initiative, 96–97
Family Independence Agency (FIA), 64, 67
Farm Bill
    Food Stamp Program access, 103–105
    fruit/vegetable budget increase, 105–106

Finance Committee bills, 81, 83
Flat Broke with Children: Women in the Age of Welfare Reform (Hays), 46, 48
Fleischer, Ari, 81
Florida State University, 26
Food, Nutrition and Consumer Services (FNCS), 98
Food and Nutrition Service (FNS), 100, 102
Food Stamp Act of 1977, 103
Food Stamp block grant, 87
Food Stamp Nutrition Connection (Web site), 103
Food Stamp Nutrition Education (FSNE), 102
Food Stamp Program (FSP)
    benefits for low-income families, 98–99
    fruit/vegetables, need for budgetary increases, 105–106
    increasing access to, 104–105
    outreach programs, 100
    redefining, 44–45
    success of, 99
    work requirements, 90, 91
    See also Child Nutrition Programs (CNP); Special Supplemental Nutrition Program for Women, Infants, and Children (WIC); Summer Food Service Program (SFSP)
Food stamps
    critical need, 34, 35
    nutrition assistance programs for recipients, 102–104
    reductions, 37, 40

G

Gingrich, Newt, 80, 90, 91
Gold, Sarah T., 44
Goss, Porter, 90

Govenar, Alan, 70–78
Gramm, Phil, 80, 81, 86
Granger, Charlie, 73
Grossman, Jim, 84
Growing Up with a Single Parent (McLanahan and Sandefur), 38

H

Hamer, Fannie Lou, 72
Handicapped on welfare, 66, 67
Haskins, Ron, 79–92
Hays, Sharon, 46–56
Health/medical care
    inadequate, 39, 54, 56
    nationalization, 78
Hensley, Rebecca, 26–30
Heritage Foundation, 88
HHS. *See* U.S. Department of Health and Human Services (HHS)
Hobson, David, 89
Holcomb, Pamela, 57, 58
House-Senate conference, 79, 84, 86
Housing
    inadequate, 16–21, 37, 38
    shortages, 54, 78
    subsidized, 27
    workers' rights regarding, 71–72
Hustling, for survival
    African American perspective, 31–34
    racial differences, 28–30
    white, middle-class perspective, 26–28

I

Illness, and welfare children, 37, 55
Income
    inadequate, 40, 51, 54, 98

Welfare

reporting to welfare, 22–23, 37
single-parent households, 38
Ireland, Patricia, 76

J

Jameson, Booth, 87
Job requirements. *See* Employment
Johner, Nancy Montanez, 98–106
Johnson, Nancy, 84, 85
Judicial system
    welfare recipients and, 23–25, 70
    workers' rights and, 71–72
Justice
    for black students/workers, 72
    fighting for, 78
    See also Welfare Workers for Justice

K

Kasich, John, 90
Kasich amendment, 90, 91
Kless, Kiki, 88
Kramer, Marian, 70–78

L

Lank, Heather, 82
Lawrence Livermore Lab, 23
League of Revolutionary Black Workers, 72
Leavitt, Mike, 82, 83, 84
Leonard, Paul, 87
Lott, Trent, 80, 81
Loving Your Family, Feeding Their Future: Nutrition Education through the Food Stamp Program, 103
Low-income families
    child-care subsidies, 40, 63
    Food Stamp Program benefits, 98–100
    housing, 37
    nutrition education for, 100–104
    poor people's conference, 70–71
    see also Poverty

M

Maslow, Abraham, 38
McLanahan, Sara, 38
Medicaid
    block grant, 85
    for children, Nancy Johnson's fight for, 85
    reduced coverage, 40, 80, 85
    separation from welfare legislation, 80–81
    withdrawal, 40
Medical coverage, and welfare, 39, 54, 56
Men, on welfare, difficulties of, 32, 56
Merced County Human Services Agency, 43
Miller, Gerry, 79, 80
Minimum-wage jobs, 12, 13–14
Mothers on welfare
    caseworker meetings/assessment, 51
    employment training, 50
    financial difficulties for, 35, 36–41
    negative attitudes against, 53
    nutrition education for, 101, 103
    survival skills needed by, 23–25, 34, 38
    work plus welfare benefits, 52
MyPyramid, 102

Index

N

National Organization for Women (NOW), 76–77
National School Lunch Program, 101
National Staff Development and Training Association, 44
National Welfare Rights Union, 70, 77
Nebraska Department of Health and Human Services, 98
Negative reactions, to welfare recipients, 12
New York Times, 13
Nickel and Dimed: On (Not) Getting By in America (Ehrenreich), 13
Nickles, Don, 86
Nutrition assistance programs. *See* Food Stamp Program (FSP)
Nutrition education, 100–104

O

Obesity
    nutrition education for, 101
    prevention grants, 103–104, 105
Ownership Society Initiative, 105

P

Pagan, Ana, 43–45
Parks, Rosa, 72
Personal Responsibility and Work Opportunity Act of 1996
    difficulties, 35, 36–41, 49–52
    impact, 46–48, 53–56
    political struggle for, 79–92
    successes, 93–97
    work requirements, 12, 50, 51

Personal Responsibility Work and Family Promotion Act (PRWFPA), 95–96
Piven, Frances, 70
Police
    harassment by, 71, 72
    instigating trouble, 18
    welfare recipients and, 23
Politics
    passing welfare reform bill, 79–92
    stance on welfare reform, 46–47
Poverty
    children and, 73, 94, 95
    conference on, 70
    fighting against, 73, 85
    on/off welfare, 48, 54–55
    related work requirements, 12
Preschool programs, 63

R

Race riots, of Detroit, 72
Racial discrimination
    fighting against, 70, 76
    police brutality, 72
    See also Personal Responsibility and Work Opportunity Act of 1996
Rector, Robert, 88
Redick, LeAnne, 79–84
Reemployment Accounts, 97
Research
    child care providers/subsidy system, 62–63
    welfare system, 13–14, 46–56
Rogan, James E., 22–25
Roth, Bill, 86

S

Sanction system, 31–32
Sandefur, Gary, 38
Seccombe, Karen, 36–41
Self-sufficiency, growth towards, 51, 103
Senior citizens on welfare, 75
Shaw, E. Clay, 80–86, 88–92
Single parenting
    difficulties, 38, 50
    welfare and, 46, 95
    See also Mothers on welfare
Social workers. See Staff, welfare
Solomon, Gerald, 90
Special Supplemental Nutrition Program for Women, Infants, and Children (WIC), 39, 101–102, 103
Staff, welfare
    difficulties, 33, 49, 52, 65–67
    race issues, 28
    successes, 43–45
    uncaring/unhelpful, 39
State Nutrition Action Plans, 102
Subsidies
    childcare, 51, 57–61
    housing, 40
Summer Food Service Program (SFSP), 101
Supplemental Security Income (SSI), 75
Supportive services, welfare system, 52
Survival skills, for women on welfare, 23–25, 34, 38

T

Talent, Jim, 88, 89
Tanner, John, 87, 91
Tarplin, Rich, 86
Team Nutrition, 102
Temporary Assistance to Needy Families (TANF), 57, 58, 84
The National Welfare Rights Movement (West), 77
The White House, 49
Time constraints, welfare, 51, 58–59
Title XX block grant, 84, 85
Turner, Sugar, 31–35

U

U.S. Department of Agriculture (USDA), 98, 106
U.S. Department of Health and Human Services (HHS), 58, 86
    Child Care Bureau, 58
    staff reduction proposal, 86
U.S. Patent and Trademark Office, 22
University of Southern California, 46
University of Virginia, 46
Urban decay, 21
Urban Institute (UI), child care research, 57, 62–63

V

Values, welfare reform, 55–56, 93–95

W

Wages, 12, 33
Wayne State University, 71, 73
Ways and Means Committee, U.S. House of Representatives, 79, 80
Weidinger, Matt, 84
Welfare benefits
    employment reductions, 39, 40
    inadequacies, 27, 36–37

Welfare block grant, 80, 85
Welfare fraud, 22–24
Welfare mothers. *See* Mothers on welfare
Welfare recipients
    education, 12, 50
    judicial system and, 23–25, 70
    loss of dignity, 32–33, 75
    successes, 95
    treatment, 13–14, 50
    values, 48
    varying circumstances, 31–32, 45
Welfare reform
    complexities, 46–48, 53–56
    fighting for, 70–78, 79–92
    future goals, 46, 95–97
    problems, 35, 36–41, 49–52
    successes, 93–95
    work requirements, 50
Welfare Rights, 75, 78
    National Organization for Women and, 76–77
    organizing, 71, 72–74
Welfare-to-work
    cases, 58
    funding, 87
    graduates, speech to, 93–97
    sanctions, 80
Welfare Workers for Justice, 74
West, Guida, 77
West Central Organization (WCO), Detroit, 70, 71
Wiley, George, 71, 73
Wilhelm, Karen, 64–68
Women, on welfare. *See* Mothers on welfare
Women's rights, and welfare rights, 76–77
Workers' rights, 71–72
"Workfare" placements, 50, 51
Work requirements. *See* Employment